THE TEN COMMANDMENTS

THE TEN COMMANDMENTS

A Short History of an Ancient Text

Michael Coogan

Yale UNIVERSITY PRESS

New Haven & London

Published with assistance from the Louis Stern Memorial Fund.

Yale University Press books may be purchased in quantity for
educational, business, or promotional use. For information, please e-mail
sales.press@yale.edu (U.S. office) or sales@yaleup.co.uk (U.K. office).

Designed by James J. Johnson.
Set in Stemple Garamond type by Newgen North America, Inc.
Printed in the United States of America.

Library of Congress Cataloging-in-Publication Data

Coogan, Michael David.
    The ten commandments : a short history of an ancient text / Michael Coogan.
        pages cm
    Includes bibliographical references and index.
    ISBN: 978-0-300-17871-5 (cloth : alk. paper)   1. Ten commandments—
Criticism, interpretation, etc.   I. Title.
    BS1285.52.C66 2014
    222'.1606—dc23

                                                        2013046737

A catalogue record for this book is available from the British Library.

This paper meets the requirements of ANSI/NISO Z39.48-1992
(Permanence of Paper).

10 9 8 7 6 5 4 3 2 1

For Margaret Coogan and Elizabeth Lueke
with love

CONTENTS

THE THREE BIBLICAL VERSIONS OF THE TEN COMMANDMENTS

(Superscript numerals indicate verse numbers.)

THE TEN COMMANDMENTS IN EXODUS 20

1   [2]I am Yahweh, your god, who brought you out from the land of Egypt, from the house of slaves. [3]You should have no other gods besides me.

2   [4]You should not make for yourself a graven image, or a form of whatever is in the heavens above or on the earth beneath or in the waters under the earth. [5]You should not bow down to them and you should not serve them. For I, Yahweh, your god, am a jealous god, punishing sons for fathers' sins to three and four generations of those who hate me, [6]but showing steadfast love to thousands of generations of those who love me and keep my commandments.

3   [7]You should not use the name of Yahweh, your god, for nothing, because Yahweh will not acquit anyone who uses his name for nothing.

4   [8]Remember the day of the Sabbath to make it holy. [9]Six days you may work and do all your tasks, [10]but the

seventh day is a sabbath to Yahweh, your god. You should not do any task: you or your son or your daughter, your male slave or your female slave, or your cattle, or your resident alien who is within your gates. [11]For in six days Yahweh made the heavens and the earth and the sea and all that is in them, but he rested on the seventh day. For this reason Yahweh blessed the day of the Sabbath and made it holy.

5   [12]Honor your father and your mother so that your days may be long on the land that Yahweh, your god, is giving to you.

6   [13]You should not murder.

7   [14]You should not commit adultery.

8   [15]You should not kidnap.

9   [16]You should not reply as a false witness against your neighbor.

10   [17]You should not scheme against your neighbor's house; you should not scheme against your neighbor's wife, or his male slave or his female slave, or his ox or his donkey, or anything that is your neighbor's.

THE TEN COMMANDMENTS IN DEUTERONOMY 5

1   [6]I am Yahweh, your god, who brought you out from the land of Egypt, from the house of slaves. [7]You should have no other gods besides me.

2   [8]You should not make for yourself a graven image, a form of whatever is in the heavens above or on the earth beneath or in the waters under the earth. [9]You should not bow

down to them and you should not serve them. For I, Yahweh, your god, am a jealous god, punishing sons for fathers' sins to three and four generations of those who hate me, [10]but showing steadfast love to thousands of generations of those who love me and keep my commandments.

3   [11]You should not use the name of Yahweh, your god, for nothing, because Yahweh will not acquit anyone who uses his name for nothing.

4   [12]Observe the day of the Sabbath to make it holy, as Yahweh, your god, commanded you. [13]Six days you may labor and do all your tasks, [14]but the seventh day is a sabbath to Yahweh, your god. You should not do any task: you or your son or your daughter, or your male or female slave, or your ox or your donkey or any of your cattle, or your resident alien who is within your gates, so that your male slave and your female slave may rest like you. [15]Remember that you were a slave in the land of Egypt, and Yahweh, your god, brought you out from there with a strong hand and an outstretched arm. For this reason Yahweh, your god, commanded you to keep the day of the Sabbath.

5   [16]Honor your father and your mother as Yahweh, your god, commanded you, so that your days may be long and so that it may be good for you on the land that Yahweh, your god, is giving to you.

6   [17]You should not murder.

7   [18]And you should not commit adultery.

8   [19]And you should not kidnap.

9   [20]And you should not reply as a false witness against your neighbor.

10 ²¹And you should not scheme against your neighbor's wife; and you should not crave your neighbor's house, his field, or his male slave or his female slave, his ox or his donkey, or anything that is your neighbor's.

THE TEN COMMANDMENTS IN EXODUS 34 ("THE RITUAL DECALOGUE")

1 ¹⁰Behold, I am making a covenant. Before all your people I will do wonders that have never before been created on all the earth or among all the nations; and all the people in whose midst you are will see how awesome is Yahweh's deed, which I will do with you.

2 ¹¹Keep what I am commanding you today. I will drive out before you the Amorites, the Canaanites, the Hittites, the Perizzites, the Hivites, and the Jebusites. ¹²Take care not to make a covenant with the inhabitants of the land which you are entering, so that it becomes a snare in your midst. ¹³Rather, you should tear down their altars and you should break their standing stones and you should cut down their sacred poles. ¹⁴For you should not bow down to another god, for Yahweh—"Jealous" is his name!—is a jealous god. ¹⁵Nor should you make a covenant with the inhabitants of the land, who are promiscuous with their gods and sacrifice to their gods, so that one of them calls to you and you eat of his sacrifice. ¹⁶And you will take some of his daughters for your sons, and his daughters will be promiscuous with other gods and will cause your sons to be promiscuous with their gods.

3 ¹⁷You should not make for yourself molten gods.

4   [18]You should keep the festival of unleavened bread. For seven days you should eat unleavened bread, as I commanded you, at the appointed time in the month of Abib, because in the month of Abib you went out from Egypt.

5   [19]All that first issues from the womb is mine, all your livestock that have a male first issue, ox and sheep. [20]The first issue of a donkey you should buy back with a sheep; if you do not buy it back, then you should break its neck. The firstborn of your sons you should buy back. Let no one appear before me empty-handed.

6   [21]Six days you may work, but on the seventh day you should rest. Even at plowing-time and harvest-time you should rest.

7   [22]You should observe the festival of weeks, the first fruits of the wheat harvest, and the festival of gathering at the turn of the year. [23]Three times a year, all your males should appear before the lord Yahweh, the god of Israel. [24]For I will dispossess nations before you and I will widen your border, and no one will scheme against your land when you go up to see the face of Yahweh, your god, three times a year.

8   [25]You should not offer the blood of my sacrifice with leaven. And the sacrifice of the Passover festival should not remain overnight until morning.

9   [26]The best of the first fruits of your land you should bring to the house of Yahweh, your god.

10   You should not boil a kid in its mother's milk.

1

IDOLS AND IMAGES

JUNE 10, 1956, WAS A SUNNY DAY IN NORTH DAKOTA. Smiling for the camera, the actor Charlton Heston, Judge E. J. Ruegemer, and two elected officials stood on either side of a large carved stone slab titled "the Ten Commandments" (Figure 1). Since the 1940s Ruegemer, a juvenile court judge, had led the campaign of the Fraternal Order of Eagles (FOE) to combat juvenile delinquency by distributing copies of the Ten Commandments to Boy Scouts and other civic and religious groups throughout the United States. The matinee idol Charlton Heston was there as part of the promotion for Cecil B. DeMille's film epic *The Ten Commandments*, which opened October 5, 1956, and in which Heston played Moses. DeMille joined the FOE campaign, and arranged and paid for public monuments to be erected all over the country, with the film's stars Heston, Yul Brynner, and Martha Scott appearing at the dedication of three of them. So a sincere, if naïve, campaign was co-opted by Hollywood public relations.

Some of these monuments, and other public displays of the Ten Commandments, have been the subject of court

FIGURE I. The dedication of the monument of the Ten Commandments in Dunseith, North Dakota, in 1956. Judge Ruegemer is on the right, and Charlton Heston, who played Moses in DeMille's *The Ten Commandments,* is on the left. Credit: Institute for Regional Studies, North Dakota State University, Fargo, North Dakota (rs 006131).

cases, including *Van Orden v. Perry.* Thomas Van Orden, an avowed atheist, sued the state of Texas (in the person of its governor, Rick Perry), claiming that the Ten Commandments monument on the grounds of the state capitol in Austin, Texas, also funded by the FOE (see Figure 2), was unconstitutional.[1] He argued that it amounted to governmental endorsement of one religion, thus violating the "establishment clause" of the First Amendment to the Constitution, which

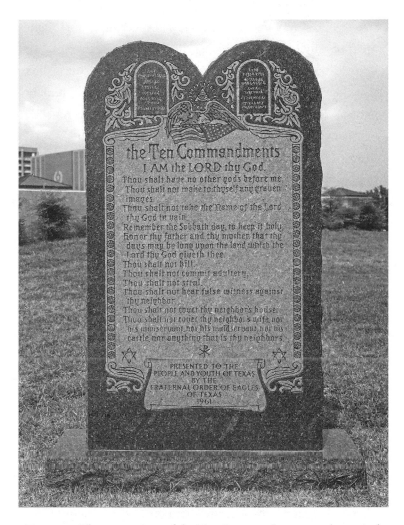

FIGURE 2. The monument of the Ten Commandments on the capitol grounds in Austin, Texas, the issue in *Van Orden v. Perry.* Courtesy of State Preservation Board, Austin, Texas; Accession ID: CHA 1989.685.

states: "Congress shall make no law respecting an establishment of religion, or prohibiting the free exercise thereof." In its decision of this case in 2005, the U.S. Supreme Court ruled that the monument was constitutional and so could remain in place, because religion in general, and the Ten Commandments in particular, were part of the heritage of the United States, and so the monument's purpose was more historical than religious. In other cases, however, both lower federal courts and the Supreme Court have ruled that displaying the Ten Commandments, and other explicitly religious texts in public spaces and on government buildings, does violate the "establishment clause." The main exceptions are when the Ten Commandments are part of a display of great laws or lawgivers of history. That is the case, for example, in sculptures and decoration in the building of the Supreme Court itself. A second exception, according to Justice Breyer in his concurring opinion in *Van Orden v. Perry*, is when the monument in question has been there for so long that by dint of time it has itself become historic, like the monument in Austin, which was erected in 1961, in a public space with many other historic monuments and markers.[2]

One of the arguments that proponents make in support of the FOE and similar monuments is that their content is not primarily or exclusively religious, and at first glance that would appear to be the case. Let us begin with the decorative frame, as shown in Figures 1 and 2. At the top, centered between the two tablets of the Ten Commandments, is a stylized version of the "Great Seal of the United States," found in its complete form on the one-dollar bill. The version on the monument combines the eye of Providence at the top of a pyramid from the back of the seal with the eagle from the front, which is holding in its talons the American flag. This then is very much an American monument, whose subject is not just the Ten Commandments.

In the upper corners, as if they were receding into the background, are the two tablets of the Ten Commandments, with an abbreviated version of the biblical text inscribed on them in stylized archaic Hebrew script. Balancing them in the bottom corners of the monument are two six-pointed stars, a symbol of Judaism, and centered between the stars is the Christian symbol ☧, the first two letters of the title "Christ" in Greek (chi and rho) superimposed on each other.

Now let us consider the text of the Ten Commandments on the monument. It is severely abridged, stripped of the particulars that make it a very Israelite text. Gone is God's self-identification as the one who brought the Israelites "out from the land of Egypt, from the house of slaves" (Exodus 20:2). Gone too are the theologically challenging descriptions of God as jealous, punishing sons for their fathers' sins to three and four generations, and never forgiving the misuse of his name (Exodus 20:5, 7). Gone as well is the explanation of the Sabbath, which in the version of the Ten Commandments on the monument connects it with the unscientific view that the world was created in six days (Exodus 20:11). I should also note that the words rendered "manservant" and "maid-servant" (as in the venerable King James Version) soften the sense of the original Hebrew words, which mean actual slaves, as the Israelites had been in Egypt; the alternate version of the Sabbath commandment in Deuteronomy makes this clear: ". . . so that your male slave and your female slave may rest like you. Remember that you were a slave in the land of Egypt" (Deuteronomy 5:14–15).

Curiously, the commandment concerning parents is not abridged. They are to be honored "that thy days may be long upon the land which the Lord thy God giveth thee." In its context on the monument, under the Great Seal of the United States, this could easily be interpreted to mean not the biblical Promised Land of Canaan, but the New Canaan, the "Providence Plantation" of the American people.

The FOE monuments, then, are hybrids: very American, very Christian, both secular and sacred. Their content and their placement in public spaces rather than in houses of worship seem to assert that the Ten Commandments is one of the central, even foundational texts of the United States, which is in essence a Christian (or perhaps a "Judeo-Christian") nation. But it is not very biblical for several reasons, one of which, in addition to those already given, is that its depiction of the eagle violates the commandment that prohibits the making of graven images.

Commercial, constitutional, and textual matters aside, there are more important issues: Is this ancient Israelite set of laws an appropriate, if controversial, American symbol? Are its values so easily transferable to a modern context? Before we can decide on the relevance for our time of a text that is several thousand years old, we should determine what it meant in its original setting, to its first audiences. To do so we will need to consider the Ten Commandments in their historical and literary contexts in the Bible, as well as in their broader ancient Near Eastern environment. We will see that the Ten Commandments are the stipulations of the contract or covenant between God and Israel, a central biblical concept that is also elucidated by other types of contracts in biblical and ancient Near Eastern law. Moreover, the Ten Commandments come from a culture different in many ways from ours. Ancient biblical society was overwhelmingly patriarchal, one in which women were essentially property and slavery was a given. The Ten Commandments reflect those values—but should they still be authoritative, even if contained in an apparently divinely given code?

We must also consider the ancient history of the Ten Commandments themselves. They are found not just in Exodus 20, but also in a slightly different version in Deuteronomy 5, and in a very different version in Exodus 34. Which version, if any, is original? When were the different versions created, and why? What does their very existence suggest about the nature of the Bible as a composite work that contains repetitions, inconsistencies, and even contradictions? Other biblical passages allude to the Ten Commandments, providing further evidence for their importance and relatively early date, but these passages have their own variations, also complicating the issue of immutability.

By late biblical times, the Ten Commandments had achieved a special status, as a kind of epitome of biblical teaching to guide belief and practice. That status is apparent in the New Testament and in other early Jewish and Christian texts. But also by then, and continuing up to the present, it is clear that the prescriptions and prohibitions of the Ten Commandments were not always observed literally, and various subgroups within Judaism and Christianity differed, and continue to differ, about how to interpret and apply them. Is making an image of God—or of any divine, human, or animal form—allowed, or not? Is the Sabbath to be observed on Saturday or Sunday? Are women hierarchically subordinate to men, and may people own slaves? Most important, should the Ten Commandments still be an authoritative text?

These questions are the subject of this book.

2

A CONTRACT SEALED
WITH BLOOD

THE BOOK OF EXODUS TELLS HOW MOSES, A DIVINELY
chosen if reluctant leader, led the Israelites out of Egypt. The
miraculous escape from slavery to freedom in the Promised
Land is the central event of the Hebrew Bible, celebrated in
song and story, memory and myth, retold for each genera-
tion. It became the paradigm of divine action—God's "strong
hand and outstretched arm" (Deuteronomy 4:34)—not just
for Jews, but also for Christians and Muslims. For example,
in Luke's gospel Jesus speaks of his imminent death, resurrection, and ascension as his "exodus" (Luke 9:31). In the
complex web of biblical traditions, however, the exodus itself is a kind of prologue. It is followed by a stay of nearly
a year at Mount Sinai, somewhere in Arabia,[1] the mountain
where God had first appeared to Moses in the burning bush.[2]
Sinai is the locale for the last half of the book of Exodus, all
of Leviticus, and the first ten chapters of Numbers—nearly a
third of the entire Pentateuch, the first five books of the Bible. Camped at the base of the mountain, whose precise location still eludes us, the Israelites received a lengthy series of

commandments, statutes, and rules, as the book of Deuteronomy formulaically puts it.

The first set of instructions God gave, and the only ones he proclaimed directly to all the people, are familiarly known as the Ten Commandments. That term itself is not used in Exodus 20, when they are first proclaimed. Later, when Moses gets a replacement set because he broke the tablets on which they were first written, they are called in Hebrew the "ten words" (Exodus 34.28); this comes into English, through Greek, as "Decalogue," a more literal if somewhat more academic translation than "Ten Commandments."[3]

But why are there just ten? Although some scholars have posited that there were originally fewer, or more, than ten, there is no ambiguity in the biblical sources: the primary revelation at Sinai, the contract between God and Israel, had only ten "words." As we will see, it is not always easy to find exactly ten commandments in the Decalogue, or to number them precisely, but the number itself is fixed. So, why ten? The most convincing hypothesis is that it was a kind of mnemonic, an aide memoire for instruction: these rules can be counted off on the fingers. But religious groups differ on precisely how the commandments are to be numbered, for the Bible in fact does not do so. Significantly, in Jewish tradition, the first of the ten "words" is God's self-identification: "I am Yahweh, your god, who brought you out from the land of Egypt, from the house of slaves" (Exodus 20:2), not really a commandment at all, and the second "word" is the first commandment of Christian tradition: "You should have no other gods besides me" (Exodus 20:3). In this book, for convenience, I will refer to the commandments following a traditional Christian numbering based on their text in Exodus 20; see Table 1 in Chapter 3.

God's opening remarks at Sinai contain striking imagery and important language. When they had camped at the base of the mountain, Moses went part of the way up, alone, and Yahweh—God's personal name—spoke to him:

> Thus you should say to the house of Jacob, and tell
> the sons of Israel: "You saw what I did to Egypt, and
> how I lifted you on vultures' wings and brought you to
> myself." (Exodus 19:3–4)

Yahweh summarizes the events of the exodus from Egypt with a vivid if ornithologically inaccurate metaphor. Despite the usual evocative translation "eagles' wings," the birds in question are not eagles, and certainly not the majestic bald eagle of American iconography featured on monuments of the Ten Commandments. Rather, they are vultures, more specifically probably griffon vultures (*Gyps fulvus*). These magnificent birds are equally majestic, with a wingspan that can exceed nine feet. Like the North American bald eagle, they are not actually bald (despite Micah 1:16), for their heads are covered with small white feathers. They are scavengers, feeding on carrion—"where the carcass is, there the vultures gather" (Matthew 24:28); that is why they are considered unclean (Leviticus 11:13; Deuteronomy 14:12). They make their nests high in cliffs, like those overlooking the Dead Sea, where their eggs and young are safe from predators. But what does the phrase "on vultures' wings" mean? The metaphor is elaborated in Deuteronomy, also with reference to the exodus from Egypt:

> As a vulture stirs up its nest,
> >   swoops over its fledglings,
> spreads out its wings and takes them up,
> >   lifts them on its pinions,
> Yahweh alone led him. (Deuteronomy 32:11–12)

Underlying this may be a kind of folklore about how these birds teach their young how to fly. When a young bird has matured enough to be able to fly, one of its parents pushes it out of the nest, and as it feebly flaps its immature wings and plummets down, the other parent comes up underneath it, and carrying it on its back, returns the fledgling to the nest. This process is repeated until the young bird's muscles have sufficiently developed to fly on its own. Unlikely, to be sure, but a charming metaphor for divine concern, and a possible explanation of the phrase in Exodus 19.

Yahweh continues:

> "And now, if you will truly listen to my voice, and keep my covenant, then you will become for me a possession treasured more than all peoples, for all the earth is mine; and you will become for me a kingdom of priests, and a holy nation."

> These are the words that you should speak to the sons of Israel. (Exodus 19:5–6)

In these momentous words, Yahweh asserts Israel's special relationship with him: it is to be his personal, treasured possession, his covenanted people. As such, it will be sacred, with all its citizens priests.

Moses then delivered these divine words to the people, and after they had made themselves ready, Yahweh appeared with all the manifestations of a storm god—dense cloud, thunder and lightning, fire and smoke, and earthquake—and he pronounced to all the Israelites the first of his laws. After these had been given, the terrified Israelites begged Moses not to let the deity address them directly any longer; he should serve as intermediary, passing along to them further divine commands. Moses acceded to their request, and for the rest of the book of Exodus, God spoke directly only to him.[4]

Before he had communicated the Ten Commandments, God instructed Moses to tell the Israelites that they must keep his covenant. Because of its frequent use in the Bible, we may be inclined to think we know what "covenant" means. But the concept of covenant, and the idioms and ceremonies associated with it, are deeply rooted in concrete ancient vocabulary and practice, and to understand it better we should explore those elements, drawing on both biblical and nonbiblical sources.

The word "covenant" (Hebrew *berit*) is a legal term, used in the Bible for ordinary human contracts such as marriage (see Ezekiel 16:8; Malachi 2:14; Proverbs 2:17) and debt slavery (see Job 41:4). It is also used for another kind of contract, which we call a treaty. In ancient treaties, kings made commitments of loyalty to each other. When they were equals, the treaty is called a "parity treaty," and the parties often referred to each other as brothers (see, for example, 1 Kings 9:13; Amos 1:9); when one was superior to another, the treaty is called a "suzerainty treaty," and the parties—the suzerain and his vassal, to use medieval terminology—often referred to each other as father and son, or master and servant (see, for example, 2 Kings 16:7). When the biblical writers used the term "covenant" to characterize the relationship between God and Israel, they had these legal analogues in mind: God was Israel's husband, owner, and ruler. The prophets Hosea, Jeremiah, and Ezekiel especially develop the marital metaphor; some legal texts speak of God as Israel's owner; and the Psalms and other texts often refer to God as king.

The last metaphor is especially pertinent. One of the most important scholarly insights of the mid-twentieth century was how biblical writers used the form of ancient Near Eastern treaties to elaborate their understanding of God's relationship to Israel. Several major clusters of treaty texts are known, from the late second millennium and the first half of the first millennium BCE. Like other legal documents then and now, these treaties share a common template—boilerplate, in legal speak. The template includes the following elements:

- Identification of the two parties to the agreement; in suzerainty treaties emphasis is on the more powerful ruler.
- A historical summary of the relationship between the two parties; in suzerainty treaties emphasis is on what the more powerful ruler has done for his vassal.
- A list of the obligations that the treaty imposes on both parties, especially on the vassal; these require loy-

alty to the suzerain and prohibit actions against other vassals of the suzerain.

• The invocation of the gods of both parties as witnesses; in the ancient world, the sacred and the secular were intertwined.

• Curses that the gods will bring down if the terms of the treaty are not kept, and blessings that the gods will bestow if they are. (A sample of an ancient treaty is reproduced at the end of this book.)

Echoes of these elements are found throughout the Bible, including in the Ten Commandments. They begin with Yahweh identifying himself briefly, followed by a summary of what he had done for the Israelites: "I am Yahweh, your god, who brought you out from the land of Egypt, from the house of slaves" (Exodus 20:2). There follow stipulations of what Yahweh requires from the Israelites, in two categories: their obligations of absolute loyalty to God, their suzerain as it were, and their obligations to each other, their fellow vassals as it were. Embedded in the commandments are hints of punishments from Yahweh if the Israelites do not keep them and rewards if they do. ". . . punishing . . . to three and four generations . . . but showing steadfast love to thousands of generations of those who love me and keep my commandments," and "so that your days may be long on the land that the Yahweh, your god, is giving to you" (Exodus 20:5–6, 12).

In the book of Deuteronomy, couched as Moses's farewell address to the Israelites shortly before his death, we find a retrospective summary of all that precedes it in the Pentateuch—hence its name, which is derived from Greek, meaning "second law." In actuality, the book is the earliest extended biblical commentary, found in the Bible itself. Deuteronomy makes explicit the status of the Ten Commandments as the text of the contract or covenant between God and Israel. On the mountain, Moses tells the Israelites, Yahweh "declared to you his covenant, which he commanded you to observe, the ten words" (Deuteronomy 4:13). Like suzerains in treaties, he speaks them himself, at least for a bit—"Then God spoke all these words" (Exodus 20:1). Deuteronomy elaborates: "Yahweh spoke to you face to face on the mountain from the midst of the fire" (Deuteronomy 5:4; see also 4:11–12). But in the text of the Ten Commandments we find God speaking in the first person only in the first two; in the rest, he is spoken about, as if by someone else. Who might that be? Why Moses himself, of course—the next verse in Deuteronomy qualifies the direct contact of the people with God: "At that time I was standing between Yahweh and you, to announce to you Yahweh's words, because you were afraid of the fire, and did not go up the mountain" (Deuteronomy 5:5; Moses is the speaker, as he is for most of Deuteronomy). The author of Deuteronomy, apparently uncomfortable with the idea that God spoke directly to all of the Israelites, added this inconsistent note: in fact, it was Moses who relayed God's words to the people, not God himself. Rabbinic tradition recognized the inconsistency, as well as the changes of person in the Decalogue, and explained both by attributing only the first two commandments to God directly, and the rest to Moses acting as God's transmitter.[5]

Not only did God speak the Ten Commandments, the Bible tells us, but he also wrote them down, on two stone tablets (see, for example, Exodus 32:15–16; Deuteronomy 5:22). He used his finger to do so, apparently not needing a chisel or pen. This is the stuff of mythology, meant to affirm the privileged status of the Decalogue by making God its author. But if God engraved it on the tablets, or even just wrote it, he is not a very good writer, nor is he a very good lawmaker. He switches from first person to third person, he is somewhat repetitious, and he digresses, often at length. If he had wanted these laws to be universally applicable, he could have stated them without the cultural specifics that permeate the Decalogue, and more generally, like the Four Noble Truths of Buddhism or many of the Analects of Confucius, or, for that matter, like much of the biblical book of Proverbs.

The text of the Decalogue is relatively short, so it could easily have fit on a single tablet; the Code of Hammurapi is much longer than the Decalogue, and it fits on a single magnificent stela. So why are there two tablets? In Jewish tradition, the Ten Commandments have often been divided into two parts, but not always with the same divisions.[c] In my understanding, they fall naturally into two groups, the first four having to do with how Yahweh is to be worshipped, and the last six with how the Israelites are to treat each other. Even though these two parts are of unequal length, dividing them this way is a useful organizing principle, followed by many commentators throughout the ages—and artists too, as on the FOE monuments.

But there may be two tablets for another reason. In most legal systems, each party to a contract gets a copy of what they have agreed to. This is also true of ancient suzerainty treaties: duplicates of the treaty were deposited in the temple of the chief deities of both suzerain and vassal, because the gods, as witnesses, were the ultimate enforcers of the treaty. The text of the Decalogue was written on two tablets because each party—in this case, God and the Israelites—was to get a copy of it. Moreover, the tablets of the Decalogue were deposited in the "ark of the covenant," originally, as we will see, a kind of sacred safe-deposit box kept in the innermost sanctum of an Israelite shrine.[7] Some treaties also specify that they are to be read aloud publicly at regular intervals. So too, according to Deuteronomy, the divinely given law was to be read "every seven years . . . at the festival of Booths . . . before all Israel . . . men, women, and children" (Deuteronomy 31:10–12).

Another connection between ancient treaties and God's covenant with Israel is worth noting. The Hebrew idiom for "making a covenant" is, literally, "cutting a covenant." One reason for this may be that covenant ceremonies could involve animal sacrifices. We find a messy example in the account of the ratification of the Sinai covenant in Exodus:

> Moses sent the young men of the sons of Israel, and they offered burnt offerings, and offered well-being sacrifices of bulls to Yahweh. Then Moses took half of the blood and put it in bowls, and half of the blood he sprinkled on the altar. Then he took the book of the covenant, and he read it in the hearing of the people.

And they said, "All that Yahweh has spoken we will
do, and we will listen." Then Moses took the blood,
and he sprinkled it on the people, and he said, "Behold
the blood of the covenant that Yahweh has cut with
you, according to all these words." (Exodus 24:5–8)[8]

In this case, animals were cut up for the sacrifice that accom-
panied the "cutting" of the covenant, and deity and people
were symbolically united by being sprinkled with bulls'
blood.

Further explanation for the idiom of "cutting" a covenant comes from other treaty texts. An eighth-century BCE
treaty from Syria records a series of actions symbolizing what
would happen to the vassal, Matiel, king of Arpad, if he violated the treaty:

As this wax is burned in fire, so may Matiel be burned
in fire. And as this bow and these arrows are broken,
so may [the gods] Inurta and Hadad break the bow
of Matiel and the bow of his nobles. And as this man
of wax is blinded, so may Matiel be blinded. And as
this calf is cut up, so may Matiel be cut up and may his
nobles be cut up.[9]

One of the rituals described here occurs in the Bible, also in
covenant-making contexts. Speaking in Yahweh's name, the
prophet Jeremiah pronounced judgment on his contemporaries who had not lived up to the terms of the covenant that
they had made to free Hebrew slaves after six years of service:

As for those men who violated my covenant, who did
not keep the words of the covenant that they had cut

before me, I will make them like the calf which they
cut in two and passed between its pieces, the princes
of Judah and the princes of Jerusalem, the officials and
the priests and all the people of the land, who passed
between the pieces of the calf. I will give them into the
hand of their enemies and of those seeking their lives.
(Jeremiah 34:18–20; the same Hebrew word is used for
"violate" and "pass")

During the covenant-making ceremony, then, the parties to
the covenant actually walked between the divided carcasses
of animals. Even Yahweh did so, in one of the accounts of his
covenant with Abraham. He instructed the patriarch to bring
him a three-year-old heifer, a three-year-old nanny goat, a
three-year-old ram, a turtledove, and a pigeon. Abraham
brought the animals, and cut them in half, with the halves op-
posite each other; then he shooed away the scavenger birds
inevitably drawn to the fresh kill. Finally,

when the sun had gone down and darkness had come,
a smoking brazier and a flaming torch passed between
those cut pieces. On that day, Yahweh cut a covenant
with Abraham. (Genesis 15:17–18)

So God too, symbolized by smoke and fire as elsewhere in
the Bible, himself passed between the animal halves, at least in
the writer's imagination.

We should also note that like ordinary contracts, treaties—and the covenant between God and Israel—were witnessed. In the ancient Near Eastern treaties, the primary witnesses are the gods and goddesses of the signers, who would

reward them if they kept its terms and punish them if they did not. The long lists of witness deities at the end of ancient Near Eastern treaties sometimes conclude with the primeval powers in the universe—the mountains, the rivers, the springs, the great sea, heaven and earth, the winds, the clouds. The covenant between God and Israel was also witnessed; that is why older English translations of the Bible often used the word "testament," which suggests something witnessed. Sometimes the witnesses are the people themselves or a stone monument, as in Joshua 24:22, 27, but sometimes the very ancient primeval powers are also alluded to: Moses warns the people, "I call as witnesses against you . . . heaven and earth" (Deuteronomy 30:19; see also 4:26; 31:28).

The links between ancient Near Eastern treaties and the biblical concept of covenant are important not just because they shed light on details like vocabulary, the mention of two tablets, and invocation of witnesses. They also show that the human authors of the Bible were not simply transcribers of divinely revealed messages, nor did they live in a vacuum. Rather, they used the conventions, idioms, and genres of their contemporaries—and their bloody rituals as well. And they lived in specific historical contexts: their words, which eventually ended up in our Bibles, were addressed to specific audiences in specific circumstances; they were not, I think, consciously writing "scripture."

Nor did the biblical writers intend the Decalogue to be universal. It is rather a contract between God and one historical group, the Israelites newly escaped out of Egypt and their descendants—not between God and the Egyptians, or the Midianites, or any of the other groups mentioned in biblical narrative, nor for that matter the rest of the world. Only much later, as we will see, did some, Christians for the most part, insist that in contrast to the other divinely given laws in the Torah, the Ten Commandments applied to all humanity.[10]

Finally, for the biblical writers, God's covenant with the Israelites was conditional, not eternal: he would keep his promises as long as they obeyed his stipulations. This is explicit in the fifth commandment: "Honor your father and your mother so that your days may be long on the land that Yahweh, your god, is giving to you" (Exodus 20:12). It is also implicit in the punishments and rewards mentioned in the commandment concerning graven images: "For I, Yahweh, your god, am a jealous god, punishing sons for fathers' sins to three and four generations of those who hate me, but showing steadfast love to thousands of generations of those who love me and keep my commandments" (Exodus 20:5–6). So, God can annul the Sinai covenant if the Israelites fail to live up to its terms. This conditional aspect is developed at length in the lists of rewards for observance and the much longer lists of punishments for nonobservance in Leviticus and Deuteronomy, which echo the curses and blessings of the suzerainty treaties.[11] We also see it repeatedly in Deuteronomy, as in this passage, in which, as in the rest of the book, Moses is speaking:

> See, I have set before you today life and good, and
> death and evil. If you obey the commands of Yahweh,

your god, which I am commanding you today, to love
Yahweh, your god, to walk in his ways, and to keep his
commands and his statutes and his ordinances, then
you will live and multiply, and Yahweh, your god, will
bless you in the land which you are about to enter and
possess. But if your heart turns aside and you do not
obey, and you go astray and bow down to other gods
and serve them, I declare to you today that you will
surely perish: you will not make your days long on the
land that you are crossing the Jordan to enter and to
possess. I call as witnesses against you today heaven
and earth: I have set before you life and death, blessing
and curse. So choose life, so that you and your seed
may live, by loving Yahweh, your god, by obeying his
voice and clinging to him: for that is life and length of
days, to dwell on the land that Yahweh swore to your
ancestors Abraham, Isaac, and Jacob that he would
give them. (Deuteronomy 30:15–20; see also 5:32–33
and elsewhere)

So, in their original literary context, the Ten Commandments
are historically conditioned, a response by a particular people to what God had done for them at a particular moment.
God's subsequent punishments or rewards for their breaking
or keeping the covenant were equally historical, in this life, in
the Promised Land, not in some eternal hereafter.

The Decalogue, then, is the primary text of Yahweh's
contract, his covenant, with the Israelites, as their overlord
and king, their owner, father, and husband. Like vassal-
subjects of other kings, they have a primary and exclusive relationship with him collectively, and a concomitant obligation

to each other, for as individuals they are all his subjects, and anything that harms one of them weakens the community of which he is the head. Like slaves and children, they owe him obedience, and like a wife, they owe him absolute faithfulness. The concept of covenant pervades the Bible, as the names of its two parts in Christianity suggest: there is a legal, binding relationship between God and his people, a testament. But can we determine how old this concept is, and who might first have used it in this way? Before we answer these questions, we must first look at the different versions of the Decalogue preserved in the Bible.

3

WHICH VERSION OF THE TEN COMMANDMENTS?

THE TEN COMMANDMENTS HAVE BEEN DISPLAYED in public parks, courthouses, and classrooms around the nation. The 2012 Republican Party platform vigorously supported such displays "as a reflection of our history and of our country's Judeo-Christian heritage." But the displays are routinely challenged by groups such as the American Civil Liberties Union, the Freedom from Religion Foundation, and Americans United for Separation of Church and State, on the grounds that the displays violate the First Amendment of the U.S. Constitution; I agree, as have federal courts in many cases. I have another reason for objecting to them: the displays of the Ten Commandments significantly abridge them, and the text selected for display is arbitrary, since we find not one but three versions of the Ten Commandments in the Bible. The same applies to forms of the Ten Commandments memorized by children in Sunday schools and parochial classrooms.

We will begin with the first two versions, those in Exodus 20 and Deuteronomy 5. According to the book of

Exodus, the Ten Commandments were given by God to the Israelites at Mount Sinai seven weeks after the exodus from Egypt. In the book of Deuteronomy, forty years later according to the Bible's chronology, Moses recalls this revelation by reiterating the Ten Commandments. Despite substantial similarities, the two versions are not identical: there are some twenty, mostly minor, differences between them (see the full text of the two versions in the front of this book).

Some of the differences, however, are significant; here are two. In the book of Exodus, the last commandment reads:

> You should not scheme against your neighbor's house; you should not scheme against your neighbor's wife, or his male slave or his female slave, or his ox or his donkey, or anything that is your neighbor's. (Exodus 20:17)

In Deuteronomy, the order and wording differ:

> And you should not scheme against your neighbor's wife; and you should not crave your neighbor's house, his field, or his male slave or his female slave, his ox or his donkey, or anything that is your neighbor's. (Deuteronomy 5:21)

In Exodus, the commandment puts off limits the neighbor's property, listed in descending order of value: real estate, wife, slaves, and livestock. This order varies in Deuteronomy's version, in which the neighbor's wife is set apart from the rest of the property. This may reflect a depressed real estate market, or it may be a very modest advance in the status of women; in any case, the wife is still property. This change in order is responsible for the different numbering of the commands at the end of the Decalogue in different religious traditions. Jews and most Christian denominations follow Exodus, so that the tenth commandment includes all of the neighbor's property. But Roman Catholics and Lutherans follow Deuteronomy's version, making the commandment about the wife the ninth commandment and that about other property the tenth.[1] Table 1 shows the different numbering systems used.

Another important variation between the versions of the Decalogue in Exodus 20 and Deuteronomy 5 is in the Sabbath commandment. In Exodus it reads:

> Remember the day of the Sabbath to make it holy. Six days you may work and do all your tasks, but the seventh day is a sabbath to Yahweh, your god. You should not do any task: you or your son or your daughter, your male slave or your female slave, or your cattle, or your resident alien who is within your gates. For in six days Yahweh made the heavens and the earth and the sea and all that is in them, but he rested on the seventh day. For this reason Yahweh blessed the day of the Sabbath and made it holy. (Exodus 20:8–11)

Deuteronomy's version is significantly different:

> Observe the day of the Sabbath to make it holy, as Yahweh, your god, commanded you. Six days you may work and do all your tasks, but the seventh day is a sabbath to Yahweh, your god. You should not do any task: you or your son or your daughter, or your male

TABLE 1. NUMBERING SYSTEMS USED FOR THE TEN COMMANDMENTS

	Jewish	Eastern Orthodox, Anglicans, most Protestants	Catholic, Lutheran
Exod 20.2 (divine identification)	1	(prologue)	1
20.3 (other gods)	2	1	1
20.4–6 (images)	2	2	1
20.7 (use of divine name)	3	3	2
20.8–11 (Sabbath)	4	4	3
20.12 (honoring parents)	5	5	4
20.13 (murder)	6	6	5
20.14 (adultery)	7	7	6
20.15 (kidnapping)	8	8	7
20.16 (perjury)	9	9	8
20.17 (neighbor's property)	10	10	
Deut 5.21 (neighbor's wife)			9
(neighbor's property)			10

slave or your female slave, or your ox or your donkey or any of your cattle, or your resident alien who is within your gates, so that your male slave and your female slave may rest like you. Remember that you were a slave in the land of Egypt, and Yahweh, your god, brought you out from there with a strong hand and an outstretched arm. For this reason Yahweh, your god, commanded you to keep the day of the Sabbath. (Deuteronomy 5:12–15)

The Exodus version alludes to the account of creation in six days, with divine rest on the seventh (Genesis 1:1–2:3); according to it, humans are to rest in imitation of the divine rest after creation. The Deuteronomy version also prescribes Sabbath rest, but gives a different, more humanitarian reason: not working on the seventh day will give the Israelites' slaves rest. Here too we find imitation of God, although more implicit: just as Yahweh freed the Israelites from slavery in Egypt, they should treat their slaves humanely by allowing them to rest.

How can we explain these differences? Maybe at his advanced age—one hundred twenty years, we are told—Moses's memory was slipping. More likely, according to most modern scholars, is that here, as frequently in the Bible, we have two different sources. The final editors of the Bible surely knew that the two versions of the Decalogue in Exodus and in Deuteronomy were not identical, and had they wished, they could have harmonized them. But they did not, because for them preservation of traditions, even if those traditions differed, was often more important than superficial consistency.

The variants also enable us to conclude that the original Sabbath commandment was likely pithier, and was expanded differently by different authors at different times. The same type of expansion is probably present in other commandments, even when there is no textual variant as with the Sabbath commandment, such as the notes about divine punishment and reward in the commandments about images and parents. Another hint of expansion is the shift from God speaking in the first person in the first two commandments to him being spoken about in the third person in the rest.

To complicate matters further, we find a third version of the Decalogue in the Bible, also in the book of Exodus. In its narrative, after having received the Ten Commandments and other laws from God, Moses went back up Mount Sinai, where he stayed for the classical biblical period of forty days and forty nights (Exodus 24:18). As his absence continued, the Israelites at the base of the mountain became more and more worried. Eventually, with the complicity of Moses's brother Aaron, they made a golden calf and engaged in a ritual that the narrators hint included sexual orgy: "Early the next morning they offered burnt offerings and brought sacrifices of well-being. And the people sat down to eat and drink, and got up to play" (Exodus 32:6). The last word here can have sexual innuendo, as when King Abimelech observes Isaac "playing with" Rebekah, whom the patriarch had claimed was his sister, and the king exclaimed: "So she is your wife!" (Genesis 26:8–9).[2]

Meanwhile, up on Mount Sinai, Yahweh knew what was going on below, and, enraged, he told Moses, "Your people have become corrupt"—they are no longer "my people"!—and said that he would destroy them (Exodus 32:7). Moses reacted as he often did when God was angry: he persuaded him to change his mind, and then went down the mountain to straighten things out, carrying the two divinely written tablets of the law. As he neared the camp and saw the calf and the festivities, he smashed the tablets in his own fury. Then he destroyed the calf and ordered most of the guilty parties killed—Aaron, who had made the calf, was not punished, Moses apparently accepting his lame excuse that it happened as if by magic. But now Moses had another problem: the tablets were broken. So, following divine instructions, Moses carved two blank stone tablets and went back up the mountain. There God dictated to him the Ten Commandments, which this time Moses rather than God wrote on the tablets. Here is how the book of Exodus concludes the passage:

> Yahweh said to Moses: "Write for yourself these words, because in accordance with these words I have made a covenant with you and with Israel." . . . And he wrote on the tablets the words of the covenant, the ten words. (Exodus 34:27–28)

So far so good. But although we expect the words that God dictated—"these words" in the passage just quoted—to be identical to the first version, in fact they are very different: most, if not all, of this set of commandments—probably ten, although it is not easy to find ten in the text—have to do with

sacrifices, holy days, and other religious obligations and prohibitions, including the mysterious ban against boiling a kid
in its mother's milk.[3] This is why scholars refer to this text as
the "Ritual Decalogue" (see the full text in the front of this
book). It begins with a lengthy introduction (Exodus 34:10),
followed by commandments, most of which have secondary
expansions.[4] We find none of the commandments having to
do with intra-community conduct—no prohibition of murder, adultery, or false witness, and no injunction to honor
parents. We do find insistence on the exclusive worship of
Yahweh, and prohibition of the making of images, in slightly
different wording. We also find the commandment to rest on
the seventh day:

> Six days you may work, but on the seventh day you
> should rest; even in plowing and harvesting times you
> should rest. (Exodus 34:21)

It is possible that the first part of this verse is the original version of the Sabbath commandment, before different expansions were added both here and in the versions earlier in Exodus and in Deuteronomy.

Why is this Ritual Decalogue here? The larger narrative
plot requires that the replacement copy be identical to the
original. We readers, however, know what was on the first
set of tablets, and I think that the compilers of the Bible took
advantage of the plot-detail of the broken tablets to insert an
alternate version. Again, strict consistency was not as important as preserving different traditions.

As is often the case in the Bible, we find another ancient writer disagreeing. Deuteronomy's retelling of the golden calf episode concludes with Moses's words:

> At that time, Yahweh said to me: "Carve for yourself two stone tablets like the first ones, and come up to me on the mountain, and make for yourself a wooden chest.[5] And I will write on the tablets the words that were on the first tablets, which you broke, and you should put them in the chest. So I made the chest of acacia wood, and I carved two stone tablets like the first ones, and I went up the mountain with the two tablets in my hand. And he wrote on the tablets the same text as before, the ten words that Yahweh spoke to you on the mountain from the midst of the fire on the day of the assembly; and Yahweh gave them to me. (Deuteronomy 10:1–4)

Was this the same text as before or not? The author of Exodus has shown us that it was not, but the author of Deuteronomy insists that it was, and that God himself had written it, like the first set. Why does he feel the need to do so? I think because he was familiar with the alternate version of the Decalogue now found in Exodus 34, and wanted to suppress it in favor of his own version, which he had given in Deuteronomy 5.[6] If this is the case, then the Ritual Decalogue in some form is older than Deuteronomy.

So we have three different versions of the Decalogue, indicating that its text was not fixed in ancient Israel. Of the three, the latest is probably that in Exodus 20, because of its rationale for the Sabbath observance in imitation of the divine rest after creation. That reference to the account of creation in Genesis 1:1–2:3 comes from one of the sources or layers of the Pentateuch that most scholars identify as Priestly, dating no earlier than the sixth century BCE. The version in Deuteronomy 5 is a century or more older in its present wording, and that in Exodus 34 is probably the oldest; we will return to the issue of sources and their dates in the next chapter. But none of these three versions is the original Decalogue, nor is it any longer recoverable. We may even conclude that the idea of a Decalogue, of Ten Commandments, was ancient, but its form was variable—just as the Bill of Rights to the United States Constitution and the bills of rights in many state constitutions overlap but are not identical.

Let me return to public display of the Decalogue. Although I object to this in principle, I do have a mischievous if not subversive alternative. If it is to be displayed, I suggest that copies of the full text of all three versions of the Decalogue be posted in classrooms and other venues, to teach readers how the Bible was formed over time, and what that implies for its status as a supreme authority.

4

HOW OLD ARE THE TEN COMMANDMENTS?

BEFORE THE ENLIGHTENMENT, BOTH JEWS AND Christians believed that the first five books of the Bible, the Torah or Pentateuch, had been written by Moses, who lived in the thirteenth century BCE or possibly earlier.[1] Since the seventeenth century, however, scholars have recognized that those books were not written down at one time by one author, but are a pastiche, a collage of sources combined and edited in several stages, the latest of which was no earlier than the sixth century BCE. Sorting out and dating the sources can be complicated, and it is an aspect of biblical studies that nowadays is hotly debated. In the classic analysis formulated in the late nineteenth century, known as the Documentary Hypothesis, there are four principal sources or "documents" underlying the Pentateuch. It is important to note that the sources are hypothetical, existing only in the minds of scholars rather than in separate ancient manuscripts. Each of these sources, labeled J, E, D, and P (for Jahwist/Yahwist, Elohist, Deuteronomic, and Priestly), has its own characteristic vocabulary, style, and themes, making it possible to separate them. So, for example, the mountain on which Moses received the tablets on which the Decalogue was written is called Sinai in J and in P, but Horeb in E and in D; and the container in which the tablets were stored is called "the ark of the covenant" in J, E, and D, but "the ark of the testimony" in P.

These four sources are neither the earliest nor the latest parts of the Pentateuch. Their authors drew on earlier materials, some probably oral, many clearly written. Moreover, at every stage in the gradual process of the Pentateuch's formation, there were editors, or in scholarly jargon redactors, who reworked the materials in front of them. The dates for the individual sources are disputed, but working backward, the following is a plausible scenario. The latest is the Priestly (P) source, which most scholars date in substance to the sixth century BCE. It first appears at the very beginning of the Bible, in the account of creation followed by divine rest in Genesis 1:1–2:3. In the version of the Decalogue in Exodus 20 we find traces of this source in the expansion of the Sabbath commandment, which connects Sabbath observance with the divine rest after creation. The next oldest source is D, found in the book of Deuteronomy, to be dated to the seventh or more likely the eighth century BCE. Its different expansion of the Sabbath commandment, on humanitarian grounds—"so that your male slave and your female slave may rest like you" (Deuteronomy 5:14)—suggests that both it and P knew a shorter, earlier form of the commandment that they expanded independently; that original may have read: "Six days you should work, but on the seventh day you should rest" (Exodus 34:21), as in the Ritual Decalogue. D, of course, also has the entire Decalogue, in Deuteronomy 5; another trace of its expansion of an earlier Decalogue is the phrase "so that it may be good for you" (Deuteronomy 5:16) in the fifth commandment.[2]

So, in their present wording, the versions of the Decalogue in Exodus 20 and Deuteronomy 5 are relatively late, but they both drew on an older version of the Decalogue that they modified independently. Some scholars have identified the substratum of the Decalogue in Exodus 20 as E, which pushes it back a century or more before D. Finally, we have J's version of the Decalogue tradition in the Ritual Decalogue of Exodus 34, in its present form datable to the ninth or even the tenth century BCE. Put schematically, the dating of the several versions of the Decalogue is as follows:

10th/9th century BCE	Exodus 34 (J)
9th/8th century BCE	Exodus 20 (substratum) (E)
7th/6th century BCE	Deuteronomy 5 (D)
6th century BCE	Exodus 20 (revision) (P)

Narrative details associated with the Decalogue also found in all sources of the Pentateuch are the two stone tablets,[3] and, in J and D, the specification of the "ten words."[4] Given the presence of the Decalogue in all four of the sources of the Documentary Hypothesis, we may conclude that the Decalogue, or more likely several Decalogues, were in circulation in ancient Israel at least from the tenth to the sixth centuries BCE.

We find evidence supporting this conclusion in the prophets, two of whom show familiarity with the details of the Decalogue. The prophet Jeremiah, who was active in the late seventh and early sixth centuries BCE, is described as preaching at the entrance to the Temple in Jerusalem, warning its inhabitants of disaster to come if they fail to live up to their obligations to God, for whom the prophet is speaking:

> If you truly improve your ways and your deeds, if you
> truly execute justice between a man and his neighbor,
> if you do not oppress the resident alien, the orphan,
> and the widow, and if you do not shed innocent blood
> in this place, and if you do not go after other gods to
> your detriment, then I will let you dwell in this place,
> in the land which I gave your ancestors from of old
> and forever.... Will you kidnap, murder, and commit
> adultery, and swear falsely, and burn incense to Baal and
> go after other gods whom you have not known, and
> then come and stand before me in this house, which is
> called by my name, and say, "We are saved!" only to
> keep on doing all these abominations? (Jeremiah 7:5–10)

The Hebrew words for "kidnap," "murder," and "commit adultery" are the same as those in the Decalogue, and "swear falsely" and "other gods" also echo it. Jeremiah, then, is reminding his audience of their covenantal obligations, as formulated in the Ten Commandments he alludes to.

Earlier still is the prophet Hosea, who was active in the late eighth century BCE. In what is often called a "covenant lawsuit," the prophet, speaking in the name of Yahweh, sues the Israelites for breach of contract—for breaking their covenant with Yahweh:

Hear the word of Yahweh, O sons of Israel,
> for Yahweh has a lawsuit with the
> inhabitants of the land:

for there is no faithfulness, and there is no loyalty,[5]
> and there is no knowledge of God in the
> land.

Cursing, deception, murder, kidnapping, and adultery
> have broken out,
> > and bloodshed follows bloodshed.
> > > (Hosea 4:1–2)

Again, the Hebrew words for "murder," "kidnapping," and "adultery" are the same as those in the Decalogue.

These literary allusions are further evidence that the Decalogue already existed in the times of Jeremiah and Hosea.[6] Moreover, in both prophets, the substance of the Decalogue is expressed: fidelity to Yahweh in the ways he requires, and social order—in classical biblical terminology, love of God and love of neighbor.

The same substance, but without direct quotation, is also found in the late eighth-century BCE prophet Micah. In another example of the covenant lawsuit, he invokes the ancient witnesses to the contract, beginning with an address to the people: "Hear what Yahweh says," followed by how he had been told to act as Yahweh's spokesperson:

Get up, argue the case before the mountains,
> and let the hills hear your voice.

The mountains and hills are the divine witnesses to the original agreement, the gods who are the primeval elements of the universe, just as at the end of the list of deities in many ancient Near Eastern treaties. These witnesses are summoned to hear Yahweh's case:

> Hear, O mountains, Yahweh's lawsuit,
> > and you ever-flowing foundations of
> > the earth.
> For Yahweh has a lawsuit with his people,
> > and he is taking Israel to court.

Then, as in the opening words of the Decalogue, Yahweh reminds the people how he had rescued them from Egypt:

> "My people, what have I done to you?
> > How have I troubled you? Answer me!
> For I brought you up out of the land of Egypt;
> > from the house of slaves I ransomed you;
> and I sent before you Moses,
> > Aaron and Miriam." (Micah 6:1–4)

The prophet concludes with a statement of the divine requirements, providing a kind of epitome of the Decalogue:

> What Yahweh requires of you
> > is to act justly and to love loyalty,[7]
> > and to walk wisely with your god.
> > (Micah 6:8)

We should also note how specific commandments are paralleled in other texts. Here is an example. In Psalm 81, which likely dates to the eighth century BCE, contemporary with Micah and Hosea, we find these words spoken by Yahweh through a prophetic voice in language reminiscent of a covenant lawsuit:

Hear, my people, while I call you to account;
        O Israel, if only you would listen to me.
There should not be among you a strange god,
        and you should not bow down to a
            foreign god.
I am Yahweh, your god,
who brought you up out of the land of Egypt.
   (Psalm 81:8–10)

Cumulatively, this evidence—the presence of the Decalogue and narrative details concerning it in the sources of the Pentateuch, allusions to the Decalogue in Hosea and Jeremiah, and parallels to specific commandments elsewhere—shows that the Decalogue was a central element of Israelite religion from about 950 to 550 BCE. But is the Decalogue tradition even older, and if so, how much older?

When we look at the implied social settings of the Decalogue in its three versions, we find a society that is settled rather than a semi-nomadic group on the move, like Israel's ancestors in Genesis, or a group of slaves fleeing from Egypt, as in Exodus. The addressees of the Decalogue live in permanent structures—"houses"—that are located in fortified towns that have gates. The economy of those towns is primarily agricultural: both the fourth and the tenth commandments refer to farm animals—oxen and donkeys, used for labor, and cows, sheep, and goats, used for food, wool, and leather.

The festivals mentioned in the Ritual Decalogue are also agricultural: a spring barley harvest festival ("unleavened bread"), an early summer wheat harvest festival ("weeks"), and a fall grape and olive harvest festival ("gathering") (Exodus 34:18, 22). These are pilgrimage festivals—the Hebrew word for them, *hag*, is related to the Arabic word for the Muslim pilgrimage to Mecca, the *Hajj*. But what precisely was the destination of the pilgrims? The text is vague: "Three times a year, all your males should appear before the lord Yahweh, the god of Israel. . . . The best of the first fruits of your land you should bring to the house of Yahweh, your god" (Exodus 34:23, 26). The phrase "house of Yahweh" often means the Temple in Jerusalem, built by King Solomon in the tenth century BCE, but it can also refer to local shrines,[8] and that is more likely the case here, since none of the versions of the Decalogue mentions Jerusalem, established as Israel's capital by Solomon's father King David, nor the Temple as such, nor, for that matter, the Israelite monarchy at all.

Such a pilgrimage festival is described in 1 Samuel 1, set in the days of the judges, "when there was no king in Israel" (Judges 21:25), probably in the mid-eleventh century BCE. It relates how Elkanah, his two wives Hannah and Peninnah, and their children used to go up regularly from their city to Shiloh, to worship and to offer sacrifice at the altar in the house of Yahweh at Shiloh. This illustrates the pilgrimages prescribed in the Ritual Decalogue, except that in this case the entire family participated, perhaps because of the requirements of its narrative context, which goes on to relate how the childless Hannah conceived and gave birth to the prophet Samuel. Significantly, all of these pilgrimages were local, made to regional shrines; this indicates a time before the centralization of ritual during the monarchy, which began in the tenth century BCE.

Several of the commandments found in the three versions of the Decalogue are also found in the collection of laws that follow the Decalogue in Exodus 20. Known as the "Covenant Code," this collection in its present form probably belongs to the Elohist source, but underlying it is what may be the oldest collection of Israelite laws apart from the Ten Commandments themselves. Like them, it comes from an agrarian society: many of the laws concern fields and vineyards, oxen, donkeys, and sheep. It contains extensive laws about marriage, property (including slaves), personal injury, and other issues common to societies ancient and modern; many of these civil and criminal laws have close parallels in other ancient Near Eastern legal systems.

Like most laws in other ancient collections as well, the majority of the laws in the Covenant Code are what are called "casuistic" (or "case law"), with the structure "If X, then Y," rather than the "apodictic" form of the Ten Commandments ("You should [not]"). For these and other reasons, I think it likely that many of the laws in the Covenant Code are earlier Canaanite ones, adopted by the Israelites as they settled in the land and absorbed some of the native Canaanites along with aspects of their culture into the developing Israelite confederation. Among those laws are some that overlap with some of the Ten Commandments:

- honoring parents: "Whoever strikes father or mother should be put to death. . . . Whoever curses father or mother should be put to death." (Exodus 21:15, 17)
- murder: "Whoever strikes a man and he dies should be put to death." (Exodus 21:12; see also 21:22–25, 28–29)
- kidnapping: "Whoever kidnaps a man, whether he sells him or is found in his possession, should be put to death." (Exodus 21:16)
- false witness: "You should not join hands with a guilty person to be a malicious witness." (Exodus 23:1; see also 23:2–3, 6–8)
- property: See Exodus 22:1–15.

Although these laws concern the same issues as those addressed in the second part of the Decalogue, they are not specifically Israelite: they would have been appropriate in any ancient Near Eastern society.

But that is not the case with all of the laws in the Covenant Code. Some of them have a distinctly Israelite cast. For example, several refer to the exodus from Egypt:

- A resident alien you should not oppress. For you know the life of a resident alien, since you were resident aliens in the land of Egypt. (Exodus 23:9; see also 22:21)
- You should keep the festival of unleavened bread; for seven days you should eat unleavened bread, as I commanded you, at the appointed time in the month of Abib, for in it you went out from Egypt. (Exodus 23:15)

Not only is the apodictic form of these commandments reminiscent of the Decalogue, but other laws found in the Covenant Code have exact or close parallels to the Ten Commandments:

- other gods: "You should not mention the names of other gods; they should not be heard in your mouth." (Exodus 23:13; compare 20:3)
- images: "You should not make with me gods of silver, and gods of gold you should not make for yourselves." (Exodus 20:23; compare 20:4)
- Sabbath: "Six days you should do your doings, but on the seventh day you should rest, so that your ox and your donkey may rest, and the son of your female slave and the resident alien may be refreshed." (Exodus 23:12; compare 20:8–10)

These laws occur near the beginning and the end of the Covenant Code, suggesting that they may have been secondarily added to it from another source, perhaps, as I suspect, from the Decalogue itself. If so, then again the Decalogue is at least older than E, and perhaps even older than the Covenant Code.

The Covenant Code similarly overlaps with the Ritual Decalogue; both cover many of the same topics, although not in the same order and often with different vocabulary. All of the following topics in the Ritual Decalogue are also found in the Covenant Code:

- molten gods (Exodus 34:17); gods of silver and gold (20:23)
- festival of unleavened bread (Exodus 34:18; compare 23:15)

- firstborn belongs to Yahweh (Exodus 34:19–20; compare 22:29–30)
- Sabbath rest (Exodus 34:21; compare 23:12)
- harvest festivals (Exodus 34:22; compare 23:16)
- Passover sacrifice (Exodus 34:25; compare 23:18)
- first-fruits offering (Exodus 34:26; compare 23:19)
- kid in milk (Exodus 34:26; compare 23:19)

Again, these concern specifically Israelite practices and prohibitions, and, again, they occur near the beginning and end of the Covenant Code, suggesting that they too are later additions to it. Especially striking are the last three, which are in the same order and have almost identical wording in both texts.

What are we to make of these connections? The civil and criminal laws in the Covenant Code, being more universal in the sense that they are found in most ancient and modern societies, need not be related to the last six commandments of the Decalogue. But the specifically religious Israelite laws may be. But how? One possibility is that the authors of the Decalogue extracted from an older, fuller collection of laws those ten they thought most important. Another, which seems more likely to me, is that the authors of the Covenant Code incorporated into their collection the laws of an already existing Decalogue, even retaining their apodictic style. If so, we have further evidence that the Decalogue is one of the oldest formulations of Israelite law.

How old was it? In my view, based on the social setting underlying the Decalogue along with its lack of mention of later political and religious features, especially the Davidic monarchy and its capital Jerusalem, all three versions likely come from the period between the exodus and the establishment of the monarchy, approximately 1200–1000 BCE. This was when Israel as a loose confederation of twelve tribes came together, united in worship of Yahweh alone and in mutual support, or "love of God" and "love of neighbor." The foundational text for that confederation, its constitution so to speak, was, I suggest, the Decalogue—the contract, the covenant, between Yahweh and Israel. Dating the Decalogue this early admittedly goes against a current fad in biblical studies. Some scholars—by no means a majority—date much of the Hebrew Bible to the fifth century BCE and later. Such revisionism is in my view questionable, because it glosses over much that is clearly earlier than that.[9]

The Decalogue, then, is in my view very old. Could it go back to Moses himself? Moses dominates the last four books of the Pentateuch, all of which are set during his life. There, and throughout biblical and subsequent Jewish tradition, he is recognized as the pivotal figure in the story of Israel: he is the leader of the exodus, the lawgiver, the teacher par excellence. According to the Priestly source, it was also to Moses that Yahweh first revealed his personal name: "I am Yahweh. I appeared to Abraham, Isaac, and Jacob as El Shadday, but by my name Yahweh I was not known to them" (Exodus 6:2–3; see also 3:13–15).[10] In other words, something radically new happened with Moses.

Historically we can only guess what that might have been. The Bible relates how Moses, born in Egypt and with an Egyptian name, fled the Pharaoh's jurisdiction and settled in Midian, east of the Red Sea. There he married Zipporah, the daughter of Jethro, the priest of Midian.[11] We have a tantalizing fragment of information about Midian from two Egyptian sources of the fourteenth and thirteenth centuries, which mention a place called "Yahu" in that region, home to itinerant herders. Quite possibly this is the same name as that of Israel's god; if so, then Moses converted, so to speak, to his father-in-law's religion, adopting its deity Yahweh as his own; this would explain why in the Bible something new is associated with Moses.

In any case, Moses, the human leader of the exodus, introduced his followers to the worship of this new deity, whom they too adopted. Piling conjecture on conjecture, I would further suggest that not only was Moses the founder of Yahwism, but he also introduced its distinctive formulation: there was a contract, a covenant, between this new deity and his people: they were to worship only him, and to be loyal to each other. Although the language of covenant echoes ancient Near Eastern treaties and other texts, no nonbiblical source applies this language to the relationship between a deity and a people or nation. Certainly biblical tradition links the Decalogue with Moses, and sets it apart from the other laws given at Sinai:

> These words Yahweh spoke to your entire assembly on the mountain, from the midst of the fire, the cloud, and the thick darkness, in a loud voice. He added no more, and he wrote them on the two stone tablets and he gave them to me. (Deuteronomy 5:22)

In my view, then, the Decalogue is very ancient, older than its expansions in the redacted biblical sources, and the covenant that it formulates, and perhaps even the formulation as ten short commandments, is the essence of the teaching of Moses himself. This would explain its priority in biblical tradition and beyond.

5

ORIGINAL MEANINGS

What do the decrees, the statutes, and the ordinances mean?
—Deuteronomy 6:20

ACCORDING TO THE BOOK OF DEUTERONOMY, MOSES anticipated that the divinely given laws that he was passing on to the Israelites would need to be explained. That process of interpretation begins in the Bible itself, and has continued ever since. Because the Decalogue is an ancient text, probably very ancient, part of the process involves figuring out what it originally meant; only then can we begin to assess its relevance for today. In this chapter, we will examine each of the commandments with this in mind; as we do so, we will see that their original meanings are not necessarily what we may at first think. Our base text will be the version in Exodus 20, following the numbering given in Table 1 (Chapter 3).

We should note first to whom the commandments are addressed. Grammatically the verbs and pronouns in the Decalogue referring to its audience are all masculine in form. Although the masculine could theoretically be inclusive, so that all the Israelites are implicitly being addressed, that is not the case here, because those being addressed have wives, but not husbands. So, although all the Israelites were standing at Sinai, actually the Decalogue is addressed only to Israelite males, and adult males at that: they have sons and daughters as well as wives.

The last six commandments, to which we will soon turn, deal with obligations and prohibitions among the men who are its addressees; as such these laws are not especially distinctive in ancient Israel. But the first three commandments concern what a person must or must not do with respect to the deity, and there is nothing quite like them in the ancient Near East.

I

I am Yahweh, your god, who brought you out
from the land of Egypt, from the house of slaves.
You should have no other gods besides me.
(Exodus 20:2–3)

The Decalogue opens with Yahweh's self-identification, before any command is given. In Jewish tradition this is the first "word": in Hebrew the Decalogue is the "Ten Words," not the "Ten Commandments," since the first "word" is not a command. In the Exodus narrative, this is the first time Yahweh has spoken directly to the Israelites, so in effect he has to introduce himself. Earlier, and also later, he speaks to Moses, and sometimes to Moses and Aaron, and they pass on his messages to the people. But here he speaks, at least initially, to the people (or at least the men) directly, an indication of the importance of these "words."

As we have seen, Yahweh's self-identification is analogous to the opening of a suzerainty treaty, in which a higher ruler identifies himself and states what he has done for his subject vassal. Here Yahweh asserts that he was responsible for the Israelites' escape from Egypt, and so establishes his claim upon them. As the next commandment will make explicit, this is to be an exclusive relationship, as in the suzerainty treaties, for he is a jealous god, even if the Israelites have not known him before.

After Yahweh's self-identification comes the first actual commandment, which literally reads: "You should have no other gods before my face." Understood concretely, this means that when Yahweh was worshipped, no other gods were also to be worshipped, presumably in the form of images; this interpretation is supported by the next commandment, which prohibits the making of such images. A more abstract understanding is also possible: "You should worship no god except me." The commandment thus means both that at Israel's sacred sites there should be no images of other deities, and that in general only Yahweh was to be worshipped.

Although this commandment is often interpreted as a ringing affirmation of strict monotheism, in fact it implies that other gods do exist. In the rest of the ancient Near East, as in the classical world, polytheism was the norm. The high god ruled over a pantheon, an assembly of gods, and the complicated interrelationships among its members were the stuff of myth and ritual. Although each individual and each social and political entity—families, cities, nations—had their own special patron god or goddess, that did not mean that they worshipped that deity exclusively. Because the world was under the control of an assortment of higher powers, some good, some bad, and neither with absolute or enduring control, it was important to keep the good powers on your side, and to appease the bad powers—it would be foolish to ignore some, lest they become jealous or angry. Nebuchadrezzar's Babylon, for example, had several dozen temples to various deities, the most important of which was dedicated to its patron, the storm god Marduk.

Much the same was true in ancient Israel. The biblical writers seem to have accepted, at least as a literary convention, the notion of a pantheon. We find scattered throughout the Bible references to other divine beings who form part of Yahweh's entourage. They are "the host of heaven," his heavenly army, who stand before him in his court (1 Kings 22:19), ready to perform his tasks (Psalm 103:21), and who, when not otherwise occupied, sing his praises, as they did when he created the world (Psalm 148:2; Job 38:7). The biblical writers do not seem to have been troubled by the existence of these "sons of God," since they were clearly subordinate to Yahweh himself, who was incomparable among the gods.[1] Later in biblical times, stricter monotheists were less comfortable with the implicit polytheism, and demoted these lesser deities to angels and in some cases to demons.

But this was not just a literary convention. Although according to this commandment the Israelites were not to worship other gods, they often did, and were repeatedly condemned by the prophets and others for doing so. We find deities besides Yahweh being worshipped even in the Temple in Jerusalem. The account of the far-reaching reform of King Josiah in the late seventh century BCE reports that he removed from Yahweh's Temple "all the vessels made for Baal, for Asherah, and for all the host of heaven," as well as the horses and chariots dedicated to the sun (2 Kings 23:4, 11). Still, not long after that the prophet Ezekiel mentions women weeping for the Mesopotamian dying and rising god Tammuz, also in the Temple (Ezekiel 8:14).[2] For the reforming king and the prophet such polytheistic worship was anathema—but clearly not for all of their contemporaries.

So, like their ancient Near Eastern neighbors, the ancient Israelites, or at least some of them, at some times, were polytheists. What is distinctive about the commandment is the insistence on exclusive worship of Yahweh. Scholars call this henotheism: the recognition that while other gods may, or even do exist, only one is to be worshipped. In its ancient context, both in Israel and in the wider Near East, the prohibition of the worship of other gods is extraordinary, and difficult to explain. Why did the Decalogue, and later Israelite reformers, insist that only Yahweh was to be worshipped? And how did this develop into monotheism?

I cannot answer the first question definitively. My suspicion is that henotheism is very old, and goes back to Moses, or to his father-in-law Jethro, or to someone like them: in the desert regions of Midian, in a subsistence economy, it might have been extravagant to worship many gods simultaneously.

An older idea, most famously articulated by Sigmund Freud in his *Moses and Monotheism* (1939), is that Moses borrowed the notion of monotheism from the Egyptian pharaoh Akhenaten (Amenhotep IV), who ruled in the mid-fourteenth century BCE. In an attempt to gain control of temples to other gods and their resources, Akhenaten imposed the worship of the sun disk, the Aten, on his subjects. But that movement was short-lived, coming to an end when Akhenaten died, and is in the wrong period for Moses. Moreover, as the son of the sun god, Akhenaten himself was also divine, so the movement was not strictly monotheistic.[3]

According to the Decalogue, then, Yahweh alone was to be worshipped, a commandment honored as much in the breach as in the observance, for the Israelites not only acknowledged the existence of other gods, but often worshipped them. Only in the aftermath of the trauma of Jerusalem's destruction by the Babylonians in 586 BCE did true monotheism emerge. To explain that catastrophe, writers came to assert that in fact it was Yahweh who was responsible for it, and so we find words such as these, written about half a century later: "There is no other god apart from me" (Isaiah 45:21). To be sure, this was not a sudden development; earlier prophets had already claimed that Yahweh was directing events worldwide for his own purposes, but this is the first clear, if poetic, statement of strict monotheism. The first commandment, however, does not say that. Rather, it insists that only Yahweh, the god of Israel, the jealous god who brought Israel out of Egypt, is to be worshipped. Even though other

gods exist, the commandment implies, the relationship between Yahweh and Israel is to be exclusive, as the opening
words of the Decalogue specify: "I, Yahweh, am your god" or
"I am Yahweh, *your* god." The same sense is also found in the
opening words of the Shema of Jewish tradition: "Hear O Israel: Yahweh is our god, Yahweh alone" (Deuteronomy 6:4).

2

You should not make for yourself a graven image,
or a form of whatever is in the heavens above or on the
earth beneath or in the waters under the earth.
You should not bow down to them and you
should not serve them.
For I, Yahweh, your god, am a jealous god,
punishing sons for fathers' sins to three and
four generations of those who hate me,
but showing steadfast love to thousands of generations of
those who love me and keep my commandments.
(Exodus 20:4–6)

In the world in which the Bible emerged several thousand
years ago, not only was polytheism the norm, but the Egyptians, Babylonians, Assyrians, Canaanites, and other peoples
generally depicted their gods artistically, in two dimensions
and in three, and in many different media. In that cultural
context, this commandment is unparalleled: no images are to
be made of any divine, human, or animal reality. The word
used for "image" refers to something carved, out of wood
or stone; that is why I have used the venerable King James

Version's translation "graven image." In its version of this commandment, the Ritual Decalogue refers to cast metal images (Exodus 34:17). In both cases, the customary modern translation "idol" is misleading, suggesting that images of Yahweh are permissible but not of other gods. As we will see, however, the commandment prohibits making any image, whether of Yahweh or any other living being.

The focus of an ancient temple was the statue of the deity whose earthly home it was. The statue of Marduk dominated his temple in Babylon, as Athena's did the Parthenon. The ancient Israelites also eventually had a temple. The first temple in Jerusalem, built by King Solomon in the tenth century BCE, was destroyed by the Babylonians in the early sixth century BCE. The Bible gives us elaborate descriptions of that temple, in the books of Kings, Chronicles, and Ezekiel. In its innermost room, the holy of holies, was the throne of Yahweh. But remarkably, that throne was empty: there was no statue of the deity seated on it. In contrast to almost all of their neighbors, the Israelites had no image of their god in their central shrine.

About the furnishings of the replacement temple in Jerusalem, built in the late sixth century, we know little, except that the Roman historian Tacitus (*Histories* 5.9) reports that when the Roman general Pompey entered the Temple in 63 BCE he found the innermost room empty, as it must also have been in the new temple that King Herod the Great began building in the late first century BCE. So, for about a thousand years, Jews apparently obeyed the prohibition against making an image of Yahweh, at least in the Temple in Jerusalem.

What about other images? A thousand years is a long time, and Israelite practice was neither uniform nor static. Take the divine throne mentioned above. According to several biblical writers, it was a complex and elaborately decorated object, consisting of a chair whose sides were composite sphinx-like creatures, called cherubim, and a footstool, called the ark of the covenant. Yahweh was invisibly enthroned on the cherubim, and his invisible feet rested on the ark. We get a good idea of what this composite throne looked like not just from descriptions in the Bible, but also from ancient Near Eastern art (see Figure 3). The ark, we are told in the book of Exodus by the Priestly source, was built according to divinely revealed specifications under the leadership of two skilled artisans (see Exodus 25:10–22; 35:30–35; 37:1–9). So, for several centuries, the primary religious object of ancient Israel was inconsistent with the prohibition of the commandment. Yes, Yahweh was not represented, but the cherubim—beings "in the heavens above"—were.

One of the strands of Israelite religion is a puritanical streak, found especially in the book of Deuteronomy. It explains the prohibition of images in this extended commentary on the commandment:

> Since you did not see any form on the day that Yahweh
> spoke to you on Horeb from the midst of the fire, you
> should not corrupt yourselves by making a graven
> image in a form of any statue, a representation of a male

FIGURE 3. Detail of an ivory knife from Megiddo in Israel, showing a Canaanite king sitting on a throne whose sides are composite sphinx-like creatures, with his feet resting on a footstool. This illustrates the biblical description of Yahweh enthroned on the cherubim, with the ark of the covenant as his footstool. The ivory dates to the thirteenth century BCE and is about 2 inches (5 cm) high. Photo credit: Erich Lessing / Art Resource, NY.

or a female, a representation of any animal which is on the earth, a representation of any winged bird that flies in the heavens, a representation of anything that crawls on the ground, a representation of any fish that is in the waters under the earth. (Deuteronomy 4:15–18)

For the Deuteronomists, in disagreement with the Priestly writers, the ark was not a gilded chest attached to the cherubim throne and made by specialists. Rather, it was a simple wooden box, just a container for the tablets of the Decalogue, made by Moses himself on Mount Horeb (see Deuteronomy

10:1–5; Horeb is an alternate name for Mount Sinai used by the authors of Deuteronomy).

We find a similar tension concerning the bronze serpent. According to the book of Numbers, toward the end of their journey through the wilderness to the Promised Land, the Israelites rebelled against God and Moses's leadership, as they often had before, and Yahweh punished them by sending fiery poisonous serpents among them. When they repented, following divine instructions Moses made a bronze serpent and set it on a pole, as a kind of sympathetic magic: "If a serpent bit a man and he looked at the bronze serpent, then he would live" (Numbers 21:9). Centuries later according to biblical chronology, however, Hezekiah, a reforming and also somewhat puritanical king in Jerusalem, "pulverized the bronze serpent that Moses had made," along with other ritual objects he deemed idolatrous, "for up until then the Israelites used to offer incense to it" (2 Kings 18:4). So, even if Moses (and God himself) apparently did not observe the commandment literally, some later reformers did.

Certainly the Israelites in general were not averse to making images. Archaeologists have uncovered thousands of human and animal figurines from ancient Israel, many of which represent deities. Engraved seals, another important artistic medium, often feature birds, lions, sphinxes, and other creatures. So not only were the Israelites not monotheists, but like their neighbors they also made images, although rarely if ever of Yahweh.[4]

In its short original form, as in the Ritual Decalogue, the second commandment may have read "You should not make for yourself an image"—that is, a religious object, an icon or a statue, especially of Yahweh. But the expansion makes this less clear: you should not worship a likeness of anything in the heavens, on the earth, or in the waters under the earth—in other words, an "idol," meaning a false god. The second commandment thus can also be understood as an extension of the first: the Israelites are not to worship other gods, and that means concretely that they should not make images that they might be tempted to worship, as their neighbors did.

We are left with something of a dilemma: either the insistence in the first commandment on the exclusive worship of Yahweh and the prohibition in the second of making images of him, or of anything else, were very ancient but frequently ignored, or they are relatively late innovations. My view is that both were ancient, but over the ages often not observed, especially the prohibition of the making of images.

As monotheism developed in Judaism, texts polemically mocking "idol-worshippers" became popular; one of the psalms is representative:

> Our god is in the heavens;
>> whatever he wishes he does.
> Their idols are silver and gold,
>> the work of human hands:
> they have mouths but do not speak;
>> they have eyes but do not see;
> they have ears but do not hear;

> they have noses but do not smell;
> they have hands but do not touch;
> they have feet but do not walk;
> they make no sound in their throats.
> (Psalm 115:3–7)

We also find a lengthy satire on makers of idols in Second Isaiah, who mocks the carpenter who selects a tree, carves an image, and at a fire made from the scraps of wood warms himself and cooks his dinner; the carpenter does not have enough sense to say:

> Half of it I burned in a fire, and on its coals baked
> bread; I roasted meat and ate. Should I make the rest
> of it into an abomination? Should I bow in worship
> before a block of wood? (Isaiah 44:19)

But other ancient peoples were not less intelligent than the Israelites! They knew how statues were made, and they did not think that a statue was actually Marduk or Athena, any more than (most) Catholics or Buddhists think that a statue of Mary the mother of Jesus or of the Buddha is actually the saint.

For much of its history, Judaism has observed the second commandment literally, refraining from making images either of God or of any other divine, human, or animal form. But, as in biblical times, there are exceptions. Notable are the mosaics and frescoes in late Roman-period synagogues, which feature not only biblical scenes but also the signs of the zodiac and other pagan themes. That these were not strictly kosher is shown by later mutilation of some mosaics to eliminate the images that violated the commandment. Islam has been even stricter in its observance of this commandment, and Muslim sacred architecture does not use pictorial representations of divine, human, or animal forms, choosing instead strikingly beautiful geometrical patterns, floral designs, and calligraphy.[5]

For most of its history, however, Christianity has largely ignored this commandment. High-church Christians usually interpret it as prohibiting the worship of false gods, but not as a ban on making images of God, Jesus, angels, Mary, and other saints, which for many centuries have ornamented Christian houses of worship and are the themes of Christian art. Interestingly, in the numbering of the commandments, Roman Catholics and Lutherans combine this commandment with the preceding, tendentiously suggesting that their images of God and other revered beings, angels and human, are not prohibited—only those of "other" gods, of idols.

Again, however, there have been dissenters, notably in the iconoclastic controversy of the eighth and ninth centuries, and in the Puritans' later rejection of any form of realistic representation in church ornamentation. The typical New England Congregational church with its clear windows and lack of statues and images of any sort seems remarkably stark to Roman Catholics, Episcopalians, and Orthodox Christians. Even the cross found in such churches is typically without the body of Jesus.

The expansion of the commandment concludes with a statement of divine justice: those who break this commandment by making idols and worshipping them will be punished by God, and not just the guilty, but their children, grandchildren, and great-grandchildren as well. The promise of divine reward "to thousands of generations" hardly mitigates the injustice of punishing future generations for their forebears' sins. The notion of divine transgenerational punishment pervades the Bible, beginning in the garden of Eden, when Yahweh curses the man and the woman (and the serpent) and their offspring for their disobedience to his commands, and continuing to the destruction of Jerusalem by the Babylonians in 586 BCE, attributed to Yahweh's punishment of ancestral sins. It is also found in some outrageous interpretations of the Holocaust by a few Jews and Christians, which explain it as continuing the pattern of God punishing for failure to observe his commandments. But is any of this really justice? Not for all biblical writers, especially not for Ezekiel, who explained at length that only the sinner should die, and concluded: "A son should not bear his father's guilt, nor should a father bear his son's guilt: the righteousness of the righteous will be his, and the wickedness of the wicked will be his" (Ezekiel 18:20). Since the prophet knew the Decalogue, his rejection of this questionable divine morality is striking: for him, not even the Decalogue is absolutely and eternally valid.

3

You should not use the name of Yahweh,
your god, for nothing,
because Yahweh will not acquit anyone who
uses his name for nothing.
(Exodus 20:7)

We notice first in this commandment a change in person. Up to this point, Yahweh has been speaking; now, as in all the following commandments, Yahweh is spoken about. This shift, found in all three versions of the Decalogue, is further evidence that we no longer have its original form, and that it has a complicated literary history.

Nor is the meaning of the commandment entirely clear. In popular interpretation, it prohibits presumably blasphemous outbursts like "God damn it!," but that is unlikely to be its original sense. It may refer to false oaths, although those are also prohibited in the ninth commandment, which in the Deuteronomy version uses an identical phrase; we will look more closely at this prohibition when we discuss that commandment.[6]

This commandment probably has a broader meaning. Yahweh's name was mysterious, sacred, and powerful. One strand in biblical narrative is Yahweh's otherness, which prohibited mere humans from seeing him directly on penalty of immediate death. But, as often in the Bible, there are exceptions. When they were permitted to see God (or his divine messenger), Jacob (Genesis 32:30), Gideon (Judges 6:22–23), Samson's parents (Judges 13:22), and Isaiah (Isaiah 6:5) all survived, to their surprise. In Moses's case, we find inconsistent accounts. On the one hand, he (along with Aaron and others) saw God on top of Mount Sinai, where they shared a meal with him (Exodus 24:11) as Abraham had done earlier (Genesis 18:1–8). But later, after the golden calf episode, Yahweh told Moses categorically "No one can see me and live," and allowed him to see only his back(side) (Exodus 33:20–23).

This inaccessibility extends to the divine name, which the deity is reluctant to disclose, as in the initial revelation to Moses in the burning bush: when Moses reasonably asks the name of the deity who has appeared to him so mysteriously, God gives a series of evasive and not fully understandable replies, beginning with "I am who I am," as if to say, "My name is none of your business" (Exodus 3:13–14).[7] Elsewhere God, or his messenger, is similarly reluctant to reveal his name to Jacob (Genesis 32:29) and to Samson's parents (Judges 13:17–18).

Why would a deity be reluctant to reveal his name? Because giving a name, knowing a name, and using a name are expressions of control. In folkloric magic in many cultures, when divine beings were called upon by their proper names, they were compelled to act. In the Bible, when the first human named the animals, he showed his "dominion" over them (Genesis 2:19–20; compare 1:28). When foreign rulers appointed kings over Judah, they sometimes changed their clients' names, showing them who was really in charge (see 2 Kings 23:34; 24:17). A more modern parallel occurs in the story of Rumpelstiltskin, in which the queen finally gains power over the evil dwarf when she learns his name. So a further explanation for prohibiting the use of the divine name may be that, like the insistence on exclusive worship of Yahweh and the ban on making images of him, it distinguished Israelite religion from the religions of its neighbors. The Israelites' new god with the mysterious name was not a god who could be controlled by invoking his name in incantation or magic, any more than he could be localized in a statue.

Certainly this is the view of Jewish tradition, which by late in the biblical period refrained from ever using God's holy name Yahweh, substituting for it *adonay*, which means roughly "Lord." But because the consonantal text of the Bible could not be altered, the vowels of *adonay* were used with the consonants *yhwh*. The vowels originally used with the four consonants (*yhwh*) of the divine name, the Tetragrammaton, have therefore been lost; the conventional vocalization "Yahweh" is an educated guess based on fragmentary evidence. The pious substitution of "Lord" for "Yahweh" has been adopted by most translators, both Jewish and Christian, from antiquity to the present, and "Yahweh" is nowadays used mostly by scholars. The substitution also caused a curious error. Medieval Christians did not understand this convention, and so mistakenly read the divine name as "Jehovah," which is not Hebrew at all.

4

Remember the day of the Sabbath to make it holy.
Six days you should work and do all your tasks,
but the seventh day is a sabbath to Yahweh, your god.
You should not do any task:
you or your son or your daughter, your male or
your female slave,
or your cattle, or your resident alien who is
within your gates.
For in six days Yahweh made the heavens and
the earth and the sea and all that is in them,

but he rested on the seventh day.
For this reason Yahweh blessed the day of the
Sabbath and made it holy.
(Exodus 20:8–11)

The Sabbath commandment forms a bridge between the first three commandments, which have to do with worship of God, and the last six, which concern treatment of one's neighbor. A connection with the earlier commandments is made in passages like Ezekiel 20:16, which links idolatry with Sabbath desecration: "For they rejected my ordinances and did not walk according to my statutes, and they profaned my Sabbaths, for their heart went after idols";[8] Sabbath observance and prohibition of worshiping other gods are also juxtaposed in the Covenant Code (Exodus 23:12–13). Leviticus 19:3 connects Sabbath observance with the next commandment, honoring parents: "You should each revere your mother and your father, and you should keep my Sabbaths."

As we have seen, the earliest form of the Sabbath commandment was terse, like that found in the Ritual Decalogue: "Six days you should labor, but on the seventh day you should rest" (Exodus 34:21). In the Exodus 20 version (above), this short, positive statement has been expanded, explaining Sabbath observance as imitating God, who rested after creating the world. The expansion in Deuteronomy 5's version also concerns imitation of God, who set a model in providing relief for the enslaved; a similarly humanitarian expansion also occurs in the Covenant Code, where not only slaves but also resident aliens and even animals are to be given rest (Exodus 23:12). These expansions show that different biblical writers interpreted the Sabbath commandment as entailing obligations both to God and to one's neighbor, another indication of its transitional function.

The origins of the Sabbath are lost in the mists of antiquity. The word "Sabbath" itself is connected with rest, as the first creation account in Genesis makes explicit: "God . . . rested on the seventh day from all the tasks that he had done, and God blessed the seventh day and made it holy, because on it he rested [Hebrew *shabat*]" (Genesis 2:2–3). While many ancient Near Eastern texts contain references to seven-day events and rituals, no group outside Israel is known to have set aside one day a week for rest. So, like the commandments that precede it, the Sabbath commandment seems to be distinctively Israelite. But even in Israel its origins are obscure. Judging from scattered references to Sabbath observance (or lack of it) in the Prophets and the Writings, it was an established practice in Israel during the entire first millennium BCE.[9]

Sometimes the work not to be done on the Sabbath is specified—not carrying burdens, at least into Jerusalem (Jeremiah 17:21)—but never as systematically as later rabbinic commentators would elaborate. *Mishnah Shabbat* 7:2 lists thirty-nine categories of work, each defined in detail in what follows. Some of these are mentioned in the Bible: plowing and harvesting (Exodus 34:21; Mark 2:23–24); lighting a fire (Exodus 35:3); gathering wood (Numbers 15:32–36);

doing business (Amos 8:5; Isaiah 58:13; Nehemiah 10:31). In some biblical passages, Sabbath violation is a capital crime, for which the punishment was death (see Exodus 31:14–15; Numbers 15:32–36).

So, the Sabbath was originally for rest. None of the three versions of the Ten Commandments mentions worship on the Sabbath, although its sacred character is clear in the wording "to make it holy" and its designation as belonging to Yahweh (Exodus 20:8, 10; Deuteronomy 5:12, 14). Other texts, however, do refer to special sacrifices offered every Sabbath (see, for example, Numbers 28:9–10; 1 Chronicles 23:31; 2 Chronicles 2:4), and Sabbath worship became the norm in both Judaism and Christianity.

Sabbath observance thus consisted of refraining from work and also of religious ritual. In later biblical times and in Judaism subsequently, Sabbath observance was especially emphasized. For Jews in the Diaspora, it became a kind of portable mark of identity, along with circumcision and dietary restrictions. For the exiled Priestly writers of the Pentateuch, who connected the Sabbath with the divine rest after creation, it was the sign of the covenant at Sinai, just as circumcision was the sign of the covenant with Abraham (Exodus 31:17; Genesis 17:11).

The fifth-century BCE leader Nehemiah, himself a reformer, reports with horror what he saw going on in Judah after he had arrived there from Persia:

> . . . people treading wine-presses on the Sabbath, and
> bringing heaps of grain and loading them on donkeys,
> along with grape-wine and fig-wine and every sort of

> burden, and bringing them to Jerusalem on the day of
> Sabbath. . . . Tyrians also, who lived there, were bring-
> ing fish and every sort of merchandise, and selling on
> the Sabbath to the Judeans, and in Jerusalem. (Nehe-
> miah 13:15–16)

To prevent such sacrilege, Nehemiah ordered the city gates closed as the Sabbath began, at dusk on Friday, and not opened until the Sabbath was over.

As Judaism developed, disputes arose about proper Sabbath observance. One of the most striking is from the time of the Maccabees in the early second century BCE. Some of those who had fled to the wilderness to avoid the draconian attempts of the Greek ruler Antiochus IV to suppress Judaism refused to defend themselves when attacked on the Sabbath, and a thousand of them were killed along with their wives and children. When he learned of this, Mattathias, a leader of the revolt against Antiochus and the father of the famous Maccabee brothers, reportedly declared, "If we all do as our brothers did, and we do not fight against the Gentiles for our lives and our statutes, then they will soon destroy us from the face of the earth," and he decreed that self-defense did not violate the Sabbath (1 Maccabees 2:40–41).

Similarly, according to the Gospels, when Jesus was challenged for healing a crippled man on the Sabbath, he appealed to the humanitarian ethos of the commandment, as well as to his challengers' self-interest:

> Which one of you, if he has a sheep, and it falls into
> a pit on the Sabbath, will not grab hold of it and pull
> it out? How much more valuable is a person than a

sheep! Therefore it is permissible to do good on the
Sabbath. (Matthew 12:11–12)

Sabbath observance, yes, but not at the expense of a greater
good.

We see a similar perspective in the prophet Amos's earlier
treatment of the Sabbath. Attacking those who oppressed the
poor and needy, he quoted them as viewing Sabbath observance as an annoying interference with their usual dishonest
business practices:

> When will the new moon be over,
> > so that we can sell grain?
> And the Sabbath, so that we may peddle wheat,
> > to make the ephah-measure smaller, and
> > > the shekel-weight heavier,
> > and to deceive with false balance-scales;
> to sell the poor for silver,
> > and the needy for a pair of sandals,[10]
> > and sell the wheat-chaff [as wheat].
> > (Amos 8:5–6)

For the prophet, social justice was more important than superficial Sabbath observance.

The essence of the commandment to rest on the Sabbath
has been observed by Christians for most of their history. But
not its precise requirement: the commandment specifies that
the day of rest is the seventh day of the week, Saturday. Saturday has been the Jewish Sabbath since ancient times, and it
continues to be so. As a fairly observant Jew, Jesus reportedly
attended synagogue on the Sabbath, the seventh day of the

week (Mark 1:21; 6:2; Luke 4:16). Saturday was the Sabbath observed by the earliest Christians, all of whom were Jews and who like their fellow Jews continued to offer sacrifices in the Temple in Jerusalem, to pray at set times of day, and to observe other Jewish traditions, including the Sabbath rest (see Acts 2:46; 18:18; 21:26). At the same time, however, in commemoration of the resurrection of Jesus, Christians also began to gather for their own sectarian ritual, "the breaking of the bread," on the first day of the week, Sunday (see Acts 20:7; 1 Corinthians 16:2). This became "the Lord's day" (a designation that occurs only once in the New Testament, in Revelation 1:10), but never in the New Testament itself is it equated with the Sabbath as the weekly day of rest.

Soon, however, more and more Gentiles joined the Jesus movement, and rapidly became the dominant group. To differentiate themselves from Jews who did not recognize Jesus as the Messiah, Christians shifted their day of rest and worship to the first day of the week, our Sunday. So, we read in a letter of Ignatius, the bishop of Antioch in the late first and early second centuries, that in his view observing Jewish practices like the Sabbath was absurd (*To the Magnesians* 9.10). In the slightly earlier *Didache*, "The Teaching (of the Twelve Apostles)," written in the late first century CE, Christians are instructed: "On the Lord's day of the Lord, having come together, break bread and give thanks" (14:1). By the mid-second century CE, Sunday had generally replaced Saturday as the Christian day of rest, and that was made official by an edict of the emperor Constantine in 321.

In an effort to make it seem that they are literally obeying the commandment, some Christians have argued that Sunday is the seventh day of the week. But it was not, at least for the New Testament writers, who distinguish between the Sabbath on the seventh day, our Saturday, and the first day, our Sunday. This is clear in the chronology of the death and burial of Jesus and the discovery of his empty tomb. According to the Gospels, Jesus was executed on Friday, and because of the impending Sabbath, which began at sunset on Friday, his burial was a hasty affair. Only "after the Sabbath, as the first day of the week was dawning," did the women return to the tomb to finish the mortuary tasks (Matthew 28:1; see also Mark 16:1–2; Luke 23:56–24:1). According to the Gospels, they found the tomb empty; that was the first Easter Sunday. The same counting was also followed by the early second-century *Letter of Barnabas*, which identifies the resurrection of Jesus on the eighth day—that is, after the seventh—as a kind of new creation (15:8–9).[11]

While some Christians' insistence that in fact Sunday is the seventh day ignores the biblical calendar, it also reveals a concern that the commandment be obeyed literally. That same concern also motivates some Christian groups—most notably the Seventh-day Adventists—to return to the Sabbath, Saturday, as the day of rest, because, they argue, nowhere in the New Testament is that divine specification changed. The gratuitous change in the *Baltimore Catechism* of "Sabbath" to "the Lord's day" further illustrates the embarrassment occasioned by the shift of the day of rest from Saturday to Sunday.

This is perhaps a minor technical point, but it at least illustrates the failure of Christianity to observe all of the injunctions of the Decalogue literally. The Qur'an does not specify a particular day of the week as the day of rest. It refers to the "day of assembly" (*yawm al-jum'ah*; 62:9), which in most Muslim countries is Friday; but observance of Friday as a weekly holiday is not universal in Islam.

The Sabbath commandment thus concludes the series of distinctively Israelite commands having to do with worship of Yahweh. But in its mention of rest for all—extended family, slaves, resident aliens, even livestock—and especially in Deuteronomy's focus on slaves, the commandment also looks forward to those that follow, which have to do with treatment of fellow Israelites.

The last six commandments have to do with life in the Israelite community. Their requirements and prohibitions are essential for any society, as parallels to all of them in ancient and modern legal systems show. Thus, by themselves, there is nothing explicitly religious about them. But like other ancient laws, both biblical and nonbiblical, they have a religious dimension. In Israel especially, which was frequently described as Yahweh's own people, anything that destroyed the fabric of the community that he had created was not just a civil crime, but a sin, an offense against God, who would punish the perpetrator. So, the last six commandments are not just secular, civil laws, but sacred ones as well.

5

Honor your father and your mother
so that your days may be long on the land that Yahweh, your
god, is giving to you.
(Exodus 20:12)

Only this commandment and the preceding one about the Sabbath are stated positively, and like the commandment about images, this one promises rewards for keeping it. Often abridged to "honor your father and your mother," which may be its original short form, it has often been interpreted as meaning that young children should obey their parents.[12] But like the other commandments, it is addressed to adult Israelite males, so its original sense was that even in their old age parents are to be shown the respect due to them as heads of the family.

Other biblical passages expand on this requirement:

You should rise before the elderly, and show respect to the old. (Leviticus 19:32)
Listen to your father: it is he who begot you;
                    and do not despise your mother when
                    she is old. (Proverbs 23:22)
My son, take care of your father when he is old,
                    and do not grieve him during his life.
Even if he loses his faculties, have patience,
                    and do not dishonor him while you have
                    all your strength. . . .
Whoever abandons a father is like a blasphemer,
                    and whoever provokes his mother is
                    cursed by the Lord. (Sirach 3:12–13)

Laws outside the Decalogue further elaborate what dishonoring parents meant:

> Whoever strikes father or mother should be put to death. . . . Whoever curses father or mother should be put to death. (Exodus 21:15, 17)

"Striking" means causing serious bodily harm, and "cursing" probably means asking a deity to do harm, although it may have the broader sense of dishonoring. The book of Deuteronomy has an extended case law that illustrates the latter:

> If a man has a stubborn and rebellious son who does not listen to the voice of his father or to the voice of his mother, and even when they discipline him he does not listen to them, then his father and his mother should take hold of him and bring him out to the elders of his city, at the gate of that place, and they should say to the elders of his city: "This son of ours is stubborn and rebellious. He does not listen to our voice. He is foolish and a drunkard." Then all the men of his city should stone him to death. Thus you will remove the evil from your midst, and all Israel will hear and be afraid. (Deuteronomy 21.18-21)

The book of Proverbs also repeatedly condemns disrespectful treatment of parents; here is one example:

> Whoever deals violently with his father or forces his
>> mother to flee
>>> is a son who brings shame and disgrace.
>>> (Proverbs 19:26)

These texts, from different periods in biblical history, illustrate the nuclear family's centrality in ancient Israel. Each family unit was called "the house of the father" because it was presided over by a patriarch, whose authority was supreme. Failure to respect that authority was tantamount to rejection of God, the father par excellence.[13] This patriarchalism pervades the Decalogue, addressed as it is to Israelite men, whose wives and daughters were essentially property, as we will see in the sixth and tenth commandments.

We would not be surprised if the commandment had read simply "Honor your father," but by including the mother it somewhat softens biblical patriarchalism, as well as recognizing the mother's indispensability and her status in a traditional society.

We find a vivid depiction of a son's duties toward an aging parent in an epic from the ancient city of Ugarit in Syria. Dating to circa 1400 BCE, this text is written in Ugaritic, a language closely related to Hebrew, and shares many of the conventions of biblical poetry, as is apparent in this excerpt. In it, a ruler who has no male offspring has just been informed of the high god El's promise to provide him with a son:

> "Now I can sit back and relax;
> my heart inside me can relax;
> for a son will be born to me like my brothers,
> an heir, like my kinsmen,
> to set up a stela for my divine ancestor,
> a votive marker for my clan in the
> sanctuary;
> to send my incense up from the earth,

> the song of my burial place from the
> dust;
> to shut the jaws of my abusers,
> to drive off my oppressors;
> to hold my hand when I am drunk,
> to support me when I am full of wine;
> to eat my grain-offering in the temple of Baal,
> my portion in the temple of El;
> to patch my roof when it gets muddy,
> to wash my clothes when they get
> dirty." (*Aqhat* 1.2.12–23)

An adult son is to care for his aging father's needs, first in this life: providing clothing and shelter and social and physical support, and performing appropriate rituals on his behalf. But the son's responsibilities do not end at the parent's death; they include performing the appropriate burial ceremonies. In the underworld, Sheol, to which all went—rich and poor, kings and slaves alike—the dead lived a shadowy, unpleasant existence, and there, for a while at least, they needed to be fed. Evidence for this is found both in food deposits in tombs, and also in the Bible. Deuteronomy prohibits the use of tithed produce to feed the dead, but not the practice itself (Deuteronomy 26:14), and in Tobias's Polonius-like advice to his son, he urges him to "place your loaves on the grave of the righteous, but give nothing to sinners" (Tobit 4:17). So, in ancient Israel, honoring one's parents may also have included providing for their needs after death.

The commandment concludes with an expansion promising long life to those who keep it, and also implies that continued possession of the Promised Land depends on its observance. While this is the subtext of the entire Decalogue, it is elaborated only here, echoing the blessings and curses section of the suzerainty treaties that we have interpreted as a model for Israel's covenant with God.

The location of this commandment immediately after those concerning God also suggests its importance along with that of the family structure. All this is summed up in an early-second-century BCE paraphrase of the commandment:

> Whoever honors his father will live a long life;
> > he who honors his mother obeys the
> > > Lord.
> Whoever fears the Lord honors his father,
> > and serves his parents as masters.
> By word and deed honor your father,
> > so that his blessing may come upon you.
> > (Sirach 3:6–8)

6

You should not murder.

(Exodus 20:13)

Although this commandment is familiarly translated "Thou shalt not kill," the Hebrew verb used here means "murder"; different verbs are used for the taking of human life in other contexts, whether in war or as capital punishment. The commandment is narrow, prohibiting what in our legal system is first-degree, premeditated murder. A law found later in the Torah, using the same verb, makes this clear:

If someone strikes another with an iron implement so that he dies, he is a murderer; the murderer should be put to death. Or if someone with a stone in his hand that could cause death strikes another so that he dies, he is a murderer; the murderer should be put to death. Or if someone with a wooden implement in his hand that could cause death strikes another so that he dies, he is a murderer; the murderer should be put to death. (Numbers 35:16–18; compare Deuteronomy 19:11–13)

Other biblical laws clarify issues of intentionality: if a homicide is accidental, and that is proven, then the killer is granted asylum; see Numbers 35:22–28 and Deuteronomy 19:4–10.

So the commandment's original sense prohibits murder but not other ways of causing death. The usual translation of the verb has led to misappropriation of the commandment in later, especially modern, ethical discussions. So, pacifists argue that "thou shalt not kill" means that war is wrong; this is, unfortunately, patently absurd in its biblical context, when God repeatedly requires totally exterminating entire enemy populations— men, women, and children— and sometimes even their animals; see Deuteronomy 13:12–15; 20:16–17; Joshua 6:21; 8:2. The commandment is also cited in opposition to abortion, but that presumes that a fetus is a person, which was apparently not the case in ancient Israel; see Exodus 21:22–25.[14]

Similarly, opponents of the death penalty argue that it is wrong, because "thou shalt not kill." But the commandment does not prohibit all taking of human life, and certainly not capital punishment: "Life for life, eye for eye, tooth for tooth" is a repeated refrain in biblical law; see Exodus 21:23–25; Leviticus 24:19–21; Deuteronomy 19:21. In general, this is a sublime principle: the punishment should fit the crime, and in capital cases that means death. Biblical law imposes the death penalty for many offenses. Conviction of a capital crime required the testimony of at least two witnesses. The usual mode of execution was by stoning. As in Shirley Jackson's horror story "The Lottery," the entire community participated in the execution, thus accepting collective responsibility that justice was being served:

> Someone should be put to death on the testimony of
> two or three witnesses; he should not be put to death
> on the testimony of one. The hands of the witnesses
> should be the first to put him to death, and then the
> hands of all the people. (Deuteronomy 17:6–7; see also
> 19:15–20)

In that specific law, the crime was idolatry, but execution by stoning is also prescribed for adultery (for example, Deuteronomy 22:22–24), blasphemy (Leviticus 24:16), and Sabbath violation (Numbers 15:32–36) and was in fact the usual method. Execution by burning was also used, especially for sexual crimes, including prostitution (Genesis 38:24; Leviticus 21:9), incest (Leviticus 20:14), and also sometimes adultery (Judges 15:6).

Execution of convicted criminals, especially murderers, is still on the books in a majority of jurisdictions in the United

States, although much of the rest of the world no longer practices capital punishment, and the European Union, for example, has abolished it. Proponents of capital punishment find
support in the Bible's "life for life" phrase, arguing that the
punishment should fit the crime, but few would follow the
other provisions of that law of precisely retributive justice,
or talion: "Eye for eye, tooth for tooth, hand for hand, foot
for foot, burn for burn, wound for wound, bruise for bruise"
(Exodus 21:24–25). In most of the world, literal application
of such retribution would be considered cruel and inhumane.
The fact that the Bible prescribes it does not make it right—
and, in my view, the same applies to capital punishment.

7
You should not commit adultery.
(Exodus 20:14)

This commandment is often interpreted as a sweeping statement about sexual morality. An extreme example is found
in the *Catechism of the Catholic Church*, which includes as
"offenses" against this commandment masturbation, for-
nication, pornography, prostitution, rape, homosexuality,
contraception, and artificial insemination, as well as divorce,
polygamy, incest, and, of course, adultery.[15] While some of
these "offenses" are condemned in the Bible, others, notably
polygamy and divorce, are sanctioned, and still others are not
even mentioned.

But this commandment is not a general prohibition of
sexual activity outside marriage: it is very narrow. Because

the Decalogue is addressed to Israelite men, the commandment forbids one Israelite man from having sex with the wife of another Israelite man, his neighbor. In biblical law, a wife also meant a fiancée—that is, a woman over whom control had legally been transferred from her father to her husband-to-be. Having sex with a woman under marriage contract violated the exclusive sexual rights that her husband (or husband-to-be) had over the woman. Adultery had social consequences as well, especially with regard to paternity and inheritance. Notably, the commandment does not explicitly address the woman's role in an adulterous relationship, although in other laws the death penalty was enforced on both participants in an adulterous relationship (see Leviticus 20:10; John 8:5).

Neither does the commandment address other types of sexual activity by males. For example, if a married man had sex with an unmarried woman, that was not considered adultery, which differs from our understanding. In biblical law having sex with an unmarried and unengaged virgin was prohibited, but it was not adultery in the narrow legal sense of this commandment, probably because it was a violation of a father's rights rather than a husband's; in such a case, the man had to marry the woman (see Exodus 22:16; Deuteronomy 22:28–29).

Finally, other acts that the biblical writers considered sexually immoral (but some of which we do not) are not included in the purview of the commandment.[16] For example, having sex with prostitutes was discouraged, although it was a lesser offense, as this proverb shows:

A prostitute is regarded as spit,
>>but a married woman is a deadly tower
>>>for those who embrace her. (Sirach 26:22)

8

You should not kidnap.

(Exodus 20:15)

The verb in this commandment is ambiguous, as commentators from antiquity to the present have recognized. The traditional understanding, "steal," is well attested in biblical law (for example, Exodus 22:1–4, 7–8),[17] being used repeatedly for theft of all sorts of possessions, including animals, silver, and clothing. But if the commandments are in relative order of importance, then property seems out of place here, as well as being redundant with the last commandment (see below; admittedly, the prohibition of adultery also overlaps with the last commandment). An alternate translation is "kidnap"— that is, taking a person for the purpose of enslaving or selling him; this interpretation is found in rabbinic literature (for example, *Sanhedrin* 86a) and has been adopted by some modern scholars. The verb has this sense in the story of Joseph, when he reports, "I was kidnapped out of the land of the Hebrews" (Genesis 40:15), as well as in laws such as these:

> Whoever kidnaps a man, whether he sells him or
> is found in his possession, should be put to death.
> (Exodus 21:16)
> If a man is found kidnapping a person from his brothers, from one of the Israelites, and trades for him or
> sells him, then that kidnapper should die. (Deuteronomy 24:7)

As we will see, the last commandment prohibits expropriation of a fellow Israelite's house, expanded to include his wife, his slaves, his livestock, and other property. It does not, however, mention the Israelite himself; his personal freedom in my view is precisely the subject of this commandment, which prohibits kidnapping. Understood in this way, the commandment lines up with those immediately preceding and following, all of which have to do with persons rather than property, dealt with in the tenth commandment.[18]

9

You should not reply as a false witness
against your neighbor.
(Exodus 20:16)

This commandment prohibits the Israelites from committing perjury in judicial proceedings. We find a slight variation in wording between the Exodus and the Deuteronomy versions of the Decalogue: the former has "false" (or "lying") witness, the latter "worthless" witness. But the sense is the same: in legal cases, the Israelites are to be truthful. The book of Proverbs compares a false witness to a war club, a sword, and a sharp arrow (25:18), because false testimony can have violent consequences — even death in capital cases: Deuteronomy prescribes the death penalty for someone who gives false testimony in a case in which the defendant, if found guilty, would be executed (19:16–19).

Witnesses could also be bribed to testify falsely, and biblical writers repeatedly condemn bribery, especially when directed against the innocent poor. One of the psalms lists the moral prerequisites for participating in worship; a man should

> stand by his oath even to his hurt ... ,
>> and not take a bribe against one who is
>> guiltless. (Psalm 15:4–5)

Likewise, the prophet Amos condemns those who break this commandment, who

> sell the innocent for silver,
>> and the needy for a pair of sandals.
>> (Amos 2:6)

In subsequent tradition, this commandment has been interpreted as a general prohibition against lying, not just in legal contexts. Yet while not telling the truth was also condemned by biblical writers, the original sense of the commandment is clearly narrow: lying in court, or perjury, was forbidden.

Legal proceedings in ancient Israel generally functioned at the local level. The gates of each city were a frequent venue, where the elders of the town would gather for judgment, as for other proceedings.[19] As the beginning of the account of Absalom's revolt against his father, King David, shows, royal courts functioned similarly:

> Now Absalom would get up early and stand beside the road to the gate. Whenever a man had a lawsuit to be brought to the king for judgment, Absalom would call to him and say, "What city are you from?" He would

say, "Your servant is from one of the tribes of Israel."
Then Absalom would say to him, "Look, your words
are right and straight, but there is no one appointed
by the king to listen to you." Absalom also would say,
"If only I were judge in the land! Then any man who
had a lawsuit or a case would come to me, and I would
declare him innocent!" (2 Samuel 15:2–4)

At such legal proceedings, oaths were often taken, swearing by Yahweh, who would carry out the curse that accompa-
nied the oath. We find a formula for such oaths in nonjudicial
contexts: "Thus may God do to me, and thus may he continue to do"[20] — in effect, "May God do such and such to me,
if I am not speaking the truth." The phrasing is deliberately
vague, probably because of scribal scruple: even writing the
curse could bring it on oneself, and so a circumlocution was
substituted. The same sort of self-imprecation is found in our
legal phrasing as well — "So help me God!" To some extent,
then, this commandment can be understood as a kind of specification of the third: an Israelite is not to swear falsely using
God's name.[21]

This commandment is also the first to explicitly identify
the person to whom an Israelite man has an obligation, his
"neighbor." Although in the Bible the term "neighbor" can
mean someone of any nationality living nearby, as in Exodus
11:2 and Proverbs 3:29 and 27:10, in biblical law a neighbor is
more precisely a fellow Israelite. In ancient Israel's society, a
person had different degrees of obligation to different groups.
The highest obligation was to one's "brother" — that is, a

member of one's extended family, one's kin. Next was one's
neighbor, a member of one's people, who is distinguished
from a non-Israelite resident alien:

> You should not hate your brother in your heart. . . .
> You should not take vengeance or harbor a grudge
> against one of your community, but you should love
> your neighbor as yourself. . . . When an alien resides
> with you in your land, you should not oppress him.
> Like the native-born among you, so should be the
> alien who resides with you, and you should love him
> as yourself. For you were aliens in the land of Egypt.
> (Leviticus 19:17–18, 33–34)

In the Decalogue, we find explicit references to all three of
these groups: the extended family in the commandment concerning parents, the neighbor in both the ninth and the tenth
commandments, and the resident alien in the Sabbath commandment. Since the category of neighbor was more inclusive than that of brother, I follow well-established interpretation in viewing all of the last six commandments as originally
having to do with the obligations of an Israelite to his neighbor — that is, his fellow Israelite.

Yet although the status of the neighbor and that of the
resident alien were legally distinct, the command to love both
as oneself in Leviticus and the repeated legal and prophetic
reminders to the Israelites that they should protect resident
aliens, like other powerless individuals in Israelite society,
such as the poor, widows, and orphans, suggest that an Israelite's obligations to his neighbor were equally applicable

to resident aliens. As Leviticus further puts it, "You should have one law for the resident alien and the native born citizen" (24:22).[22]

10

You should not scheme against your neighbor's house;
you should not scheme against your neighbor's wife,
or his male slave or his female slave, or his ox or his donkey,
or anything that is your neighbor's.

(Exodus 20:17)

In my understanding, the several preceding commandments have to do with persons—their lives, their marriages, their freedom, and their legal rights—while the last commandment has to do with property. The most difficult word in it to interpret is the word traditionally translated "covet," which I have rendered "scheme against." In Hebrew this word has the connotation of "desire," as does its synonym in the variant form of this commandment in Deuteronomy ("You should not crave your neighbor's house"), so a frequent interpretation of the commandment from antiquity to the present is that it prohibits longing for a neighbor's house—that is, his household and all that it entails. Jesus's riff on the seventh commandment may be linking it with this one:

> You have heard that it was said, "Do not commit
> adultery." But I say to you that every man who looks
> at a woman with desire for her has already committed
> adultery with her in his heart." (Matthew 5:27–28)

Jesus is apparently saying not only that adultery is wrong, but thoughts of adultery are as well. From a moral perspective, the usual translation, "covet," is unexceptionable, if archaic: God prohibits obsessing about someone else's property, including his wife.

This interpretation, however, makes the last commandment different in character from all the others, which concern actions rather than thoughts. Breaking one of the first nine commandments would be a matter of law, and for guilt or innocence to be shown, there would need to be evidence and witnesses. But what evidence or witnesses other than a person's conscience could prove culpability concerning desire? Moreover, for moderns, at least since Freud, such thoughts are not intentional but stem from the unconscious, and cannot be subject to conscience.

This apparent inconsistency can be resolved when we realize that the distinction we make between thought and action is too sharp. In Hebrew, and in related ancient languages, words meaning "desire" are linked with actions taken to fulfill the desire more closely than in English. One example is found in a verse from the Ritual Decalogue, which literally reads:

> No man will desire your land when you go up to see
> the face of Yahweh, your god, three times a year. (Exodus 34:24)

The meaning is clear: when you perform a required pilgrimage, your land will be safe; no one, especially not a foreigner, will take it. Clearly more than simple desire is the issue here; hence my interpretive translation "scheme against."

A more detailed example of this nuance is found in the book of Micah. Speaking of the wealthy who prey on the poor, and using the same Hebrew word as in the commandment, the prophet proclaims:

> Woe to those who devise wickedness,
> and evil deeds on their beds:
> at morning's light they do it,
> because it is in their power.
> They scheme against fields and seize them,
> and houses, and they take them away.
> They oppress a man and his house,
> and a man and his inheritance.
> (Micah 2:1–2)

Micah, then, is condemning those who violate this commandment, plotting to expropriate other Israelites' property.

We thus find two overlapping interpretations of the verb in this commandment. One, illustrated by Jesus's comment about adultery, focuses on desire as a state of mind, while the other emphasizes actions prompted by desire. Rabbinic tradition recognized this nuance; Maimonides summarized the views of some of his predecessors:

> This commandment admonishes us not to contrive schemes for acquiring what belongs to someone else. That is what the Exalted One means by saying "You shall not covet your neighbor's house."[23]

The earliest form of this commandment may have been "You should not scheme against your neighbor's house," with "house" being understood not just as the physical abode but as "household," meaning all the property of the patriarch, including not just the real estate but livestock, slaves, and women. The commandment's present, expanded form makes this explicit. In it we encounter one of the most challenging values of ancient Israelite society: women are a man's property. A daughter belonged to her father, who, if he wished, could sell her as a slave. At marriage, control over her passed to her husband, in exchange for a bride price, another commercial transaction.

Israelite society did not differ significantly from others in the ancient Near East. In them all, while women were persons, and had clearly defined rights within the parameters of arranged, patriarchal marriage, their legal and social status was less than that of free men. A woman without a male protector, such as father, husband, or brother, was at risk—hence the repeated injunctions in the Bible and throughout the ancient Near East to take special care of widows. And an unmarried woman was unfulfilled, as an ancient Babylonian proverb suggests: "A house without an owner is like a woman without a husband."[24]

6

WHICH LAWS ARE BINDING?

IN THE HEBREW BIBLE, THE DECALOGUE IS THE TEXT
of the primary contract between God and the Israelites, the
Sinai Covenant. As such, it has a special status. Its occurrence
in several different versions indicates widespread importance,
as do allusions to it in the prophets and elsewhere in the Bible.
Its special status is also implied in Deuteronomy. Following
the proclamation of the Decalogue, Moses's retrospective
narrative resumes:

> These words Yahweh spoke to your entire assembly on
> the mountain, from the midst of the fire, the cloud, and
> the thick darkness, in a loud voice. He added no more,
> and he wrote them on the two stone tablets and he gave
> them to me. (Deuteronomy 5:22)

The people went on to ask Moses that henceforth only he
would deal directly with God: "You should draw near and
listen to everything that Yahweh, our god, says, and then you
should speak everything to us" (Deuteronomy 5:27). Deuter-

onomy thus hints that having been given by God directly to the Israelites and personally written down by him, the Ten Commandments were especially important, perhaps even more so than the many other laws from Sinai, which were first given by God only to Moses, and then by him to the Israelites.

Early postbiblical Jewish literature and practice affirm that special status. Let us begin with the first-century CE Jewish philosopher Philo, known both as Philo Judaeus, because of his religious heritage, and as Philo of Alexandria, because of his hometown in Egypt. He was a thoroughly hellenized Egyptian Jew, who wrote several dozen works in Greek, interpreting the Jewish scriptures, especially the Torah, using Greek philosophical concepts and vocabulary, much like the author of the apocryphal book Wisdom of Solomon. One of his treatises, *On the Ten Words,* deals with the Decalogue, which he identifies as the principal laws given by God himself directly to the Israelites: "The father of all decreed the ten words or oracles, actually laws or ordinances" (*On the Decalogue* 9.32).[1] These are elaborated upon in the "special laws" that follow in the book of Exodus, which were given by God to the Israelites only indirectly, having been mediated through Moses. Thus, for Philo, the Decalogue was paramount.

This status is also evident in early Jewish worship. Rabbinic tradition (*Mishnah Tamid* 5.1; *Berakot* 11b) reports that among the texts recited daily in the Temple in Jerusalem were the Decalogue and three other passages from the Torah that were and continue to be central in Judaism: Deuteronomy 6:4–9; 11:13–21; and Numbers 15:37–41. The first of these is as follows:

> Hear, O Israel: Yahweh is our god, Yahweh alone. And you should love Yahweh, your god, with all your heart and all your self and all your might. And let these words which I am commanding you today be on your heart. And you should repeat them to your sons, and speak about them when you are staying in your home and when you are walking on the road, when you lie down and when you get up. And you should tie them as a sign on your arms and they should be pendants between your eyes. And you should write them on the doorposts of your house and on your gates. (Deuteronomy 6:4–9)

The opening word of this passage in Hebrew, *Shema*, is often used as a name for the set of three texts. The Hebrew word for "doorpost," *mezuzah*, also came to be used for the container attached to the doorpost.

Before the discovery of the Dead Sea Scrolls in the mid-twentieth century, one of the earliest manuscripts containing parts of the Jewish scriptures was the Nash Papyrus, actually four joinable papyrus fragments from a single sheet purchased in Egypt in the late nineteenth century by a British explorer, W. L. Nash, for whom the papyrus is named (see Figure 4). Dating to the mid-second century BCE and about five inches (thirteen centimeters) high, the papyrus remnant contains much of the Hebrew text of the Decalogue followed

FIGURE 4. The Nash Papyrus. Reproduced by kind permission of
the Syndics of Cambridge University Library.

by that of the Shema. A few letters at the beginning and end of each of the twenty-four lines are missing, but the full text can easily be reconstructed. The text of the Decalogue is essentially that of Exodus 20, with minor variations, and following the Decalogue is Deuteronomy 6:4–5, after which the text breaks off.[2]

The function of the Nash Papyrus is unclear. It may have been from a scroll used in worship, a leaf from a kind of prayer book as it were. But there is another possibility. It may have been a scroll that would have been folded and inserted into phylacteries or tefillin, containers attached to the arms and forehead by observant Jews during prayer, or into a mezuzah, following the instructions in Deuteronomy 6. It happens that we have more than three dozen very ancient phylactery containers and texts, mostly fragmentary, from caves near Qumran, where the Dead Sea Scrolls were found, and from other sites in the vicinity; several of these texts include the Decalogue, like the Nash Papyrus (see Figure 4). These precious scraps of papyri show that primary texts for at least some Jews of the second century BCE to the first century CE, a kind of canon within the canon, a torah within the Torah, were the Decalogue and the Shema.

We find the same picture in the New Testament. I include the New Testament as a Jewish source, both because the Gospels are about a Jewish rabbi, Jesus of Nazareth, and because the apostle Paul, whose letters make up roughly a third of the New Testament, was also Jewish. In fact, the New Testament is one of the most important primary sources for Judaism of

FIGURE 5. An unfolded phylactery from Qumran, with tiny scrolls in it. Made of leather, it is about 1.25 inches (3.2 cm) wide. Photo credit: Z. Radovan/www.BibleLandPictures.com.

the first century CE, along with the Dead Sea Scrolls and the writings of Philo and the historian Josephus. Rabbinic literature, found principally in the Mishnah and the Talmud, comes from at least a century later; although it does preserve historical traditions preceding the destruction of Jerusalem by the Romans in 70 CE, those are notoriously difficult to extract from their later contexts. The New Testament, of course, is not just a Jewish text: in essence it is Christian, written by both Jewish and non-Jewish Christians, and ultimately it became Christian scripture, obscuring its Jewish origins.

In the earliest of the New Testament Gospels, Mark, we are told of an encounter between Jesus and a rich man, who asked Jesus, "What should I do to inherit eternal life?" Jesus replied, "You know the commandments: 'Do not murder;

do not commit adultery; do not steal; do not bear false witness; do not defraud; honor your father and mother.'" The man replies that he has kept all these since he was young, so Jesus urges more: "Sell your property and give to the poor." The man, who was very wealthy, was stunned and left (Mark 10:17–22). For Jesus, who was Jewish to the core and was called by the at least honorific title "Rabbi," "the commandments" are (most of) the Decalogue.

But note first that the order of the commandments that Jesus mentions is different from that found in Exodus 20 and Deuteronomy 5. We should recall that in Hosea the order was murder, kidnapping, and adultery, whereas in Jeremiah it was kidnapping, murder, and adultery; in both cases this may be literary or prophetic license rather than evidence for a different order, although that is not impossible. Such variation is found throughout the textual traditions of the Bible: ancient manuscripts give the last five or six commandments in several different orders. It may also be the case that in referring to the commandments Jesus was not reciting them verbatim, but mentioning them almost at random. The author of the gospel of Matthew, who used Mark as a source, follows the order in Mark in his version of this passage (Matthew 19:18–19). In the Sermon on the Mount, however, Matthew has Jesus discussing the commandments in this order: murder, adultery, swearing falsely (Matthew 5:21, 27, 33). The author of the gospel of Luke, who also used Mark as a source, but independently of Matthew, has a different order: adultery, murder, stealing, false witness, and honoring parents (Luke 18:20); other New Testament writers use this order as well.[3]

All of these cases may be evidence for a somewhat fluid order in the second half of the Decalogue, but it is more likely that they reflect a lack of precision in the written sources or their oral originals.

There is another oddity in Jesus's list in Mark 10. "Do not defraud" is not part of the Decalogue, although to be sure it is part of more general Israelite ethical teaching. Interestingly, in their versions of this scene, Matthew and Luke both omit "do not defraud," suggesting that in their view it was simply a mistake, which they routinely corrected as they did other errors that they observed in Mark. It may be that Jesus is interpreting the last commandment as I have, "to scheme against, to conspire to take"—that is, perhaps, "to defraud"—or maybe he is just being careless. This seems to be the case with his attribution to scripture of other words that are not there. In the Sermon on the Mount, he is quoted as saying: "You have heard that it is written, 'You should love your neighbor, and hate your enemy'" (Matthew 5:43). "Love your neighbor" is found in Leviticus 19:18, but "hate your enemy" is unattested in the Jewish scriptures in so many words (although the general notion of hostility toward one's enemies is). Maybe Jesus is just making it up to enhance his rhetoric, for he goes on to urge his audience to love their enemies;[4] if so, he would not be the first or the last to attribute words to scripture that are not found there.

In any case, despite some fluidity in the order of the commandments, and possibly even in their content, it seems clear from the Gospels that for Jesus as for other Jews of his era the Decalogue had a special status. But a funny thing happened on the way to the church. Although Jesus's earliest followers were all Jews, the movement that he began was exclusively Jewish for only a short time. Within a couple of decades after his death, non-Jews—Gentiles—rapidly became a majority of its adherents. The sources that we have make it clear that tension developed between the two groups, although both believed that Jesus was the Messiah. Jewish Christians continued to think of themselves as Jews and observed the requirements of Jewish law, including especially circumcision and dietary restrictions. But for Gentile Christians, becoming Jewish, and especially being circumcised as adults, did not seem essential to their faith in Jesus.

The leader of the movement to exempt Gentile Christians from the requirements of Jewish law was Paul, himself a rabbinically trained and observant Jew—nowadays we might call him Orthodox, or perhaps Neo-orthodox. Paul's understanding of the divine purpose was inclusive: all who accepted Jesus as Messiah were saved, both Jews and Gentiles. His views, expressed in letters written in the mid-first century CE, have been immeasurably influential in the history of Christian thought. He has been called the first Christian theologian, and even the founder of Christianity, at least in the sense that he was responsible more than anyone else for transforming a minor Jewish sect into what eventually became the official religion of the Roman Empire and ultimately a world religion.

Paul's letters, dictated to his secretaries in the midst of heated controversies, are often, as C. S. Lewis wryly observed, neither lucid nor orderly.[5] And he could be intemperate, as when he wrote that those who were telling the Gentile Christians in Galatia, in what is now central Turkey, that they had to be circumcised: "I wish that those who are bothering you would castrate themselves!" (Galatians 5:12). This self-styled "apostle to the Gentiles" (Romans 11:13) argued vehemently that Gentiles, although grafted on to the tree of Judaism, were not obliged to observe the many details of Jewish law, the Torah, especially circumcision and dietary rules.

Paul did not reject the general authority of the Torah; in fact, he often cited it in support of his arguments. And the essence of Torah for Paul was love of neighbor: "The whole law is fulfilled in one saying: 'You should love your neighbor as yourself'" (Galatians 5:14, quoting Leviticus 19:18). This is from his letter to the Galatians, a kind of first draft or synopsis of ideas later developed in his letter to the Romans. In the latter, Paul also cited the Decalogue with approval:

> Do not owe anyone anything, except to love each other, for whoever loves his neighbor has fulfilled the law. For "Do not commit adultery; do not murder; do not steal; do not desire" and every other commandment that exists, is summed up in this saying: "Love your neighbor as yourself." Love does not do wrong to a neighbor; therefore love is the fulfillment of law. (Romans 13:8–10)

Here Paul distilled the essence of the Torah to the second part of the Decalogue, which he quoted, and which he said is summed up in Leviticus 19:18.

There is nothing intrinsically surprising about Paul's view in the context of first-century CE Judaism. In an often-quoted story, Rabbi Hillel, who lived a few decades before Paul, was asked by a would-be proselyte to teach him the Torah while he was standing on one foot. Hillel replied: "What is hateful to you do not do to your neighbor: that is the whole Torah; the rest is commentary. Go and learn" (*Mishnah Shabbat* 31a; for a biblical precedent, see Micah 6:8). Likewise, when Jesus was asked what the most important commandment was, he replied with two quotations, the first from the opening words of the Shema and the second from Leviticus 19:18:

> The first is: "Hear O Israel, the Lord is our God; the Lord is one. And you should love the Lord, your god, with all your heart and with all your soul and with all your mind and with all your strength." The second is this: "Love your neighbor as yourself." No commandment is greater than these. (Mark 12:29–31)[6]

Both of these nearly contemporary rabbis were in a sense privileging part of the Torah, like other Jews of their era. But that did not mean that they thought its other laws were no longer in force.

Paul, however, went further, according both to his own letters and to narratives about him in the Acts of the Apostles. After his dramatic revelation from God to believe in Jesus on the road to Damascus, he himself continued to be an observant Jew, worshipping in the Temple and observing a nazirite vow.[7] But in his view, the prescriptions of the Torah were no longer binding on Gentile Christians, apart from the Decalogue and what he considered to be its summary in the commandment to love one's neighbor as oneself in Leviticus 19:18. Paul reasoned that like Abraham before he was circumcised, Gentile Christians were "justified by faith apart from the works of the law" (Romans 3:28) from which they were now discharged.[8]

Then why should even the Decalogue, which was in the Torah, be binding on Gentile Christians? Because, Paul asserted, the Ten Commandments were in their essence known to them:

> What is knowable about God is apparent to them, for
> God has made it apparent to them. (Romans 1:19)
> When Gentiles who do not have the law do by nature
> what the law requires, then they, even though they do
> not have the law, are a law for themselves; they show
> that the work of the law is written on their hearts.
> (Romans 2:14–15)[9]

There is thus a "natural law," knowable by all humans apart from the revelation on Sinai. In Paul's view, Gentile Christians had to observe only this "natural law," enshrined in the Decalogue; the rest of the laws in the Torah did not apply to them.

This concept of "natural law" is taken up by the late second-century Christian writer Irenaeus, the bishop of Lyons:

> At first God advised them with natural precepts, which
> he had implanted in humans from the beginning, that

is, through the Decalogue . . . and he required nothing more of them. (*Against Heresies* 4.15.1; see also
4.16.3–4)

But, according to Irenaeus, although implanted in all persons, the Ten Commandments were apparently forgotten
or ignored, so God revealed them to the Israelites. The Ten
Commandments, then, are the "natural law" in its entirety;
Irenaeus alludes to Deuteronomy 5:22 ("he added no more")
in support of this view. He then explains that because of
the Israelites' hardness of heart in the episode of the golden
calf, God gave them further laws. Those other precepts of
the "old covenant," such as circumcision and other "laws of
bondage"—that is, all the rest of the laws in the Torah—are
no longer binding; only the "natural" law of the Decalogue
is. The effect of Irenaeus's interpretation of the Decalogue as
"natural" and therefore universal law is to wrench it from its
historical and literary context. The entire revelation at Sinai
has been demoted, and there is nothing special about the laws
given to Moses. What really counts is the "natural" laws that
God himself gave directly to all humans long before Sinai,
which are the same as the Ten Commandments. In a way this
echoes Philo's privileging of the Decalogue, but for Philo its
special status did not undermine the authority of the rest of
the Torah.

As we have observed, the last six commandments in substance are the basis of any ordered society; prohibitions of
murder, adultery, kidnapping, perjury, and theft are found in
most ancient and modern legal systems. So the last six com-

mandments are "natural," in a way. But not all of the Decalogue is natural in this sense, as other early Christian theologians recognized: there is nothing inherently natural about not making images, even of God, or about observing the Sabbath. Nor for that matter, in my view, is monotheism itself "natural," since the vast majority of ancient cultures and some modern ones as well have been polytheistic.[10]

Ever since Paul, Christians have been ambivalent about what they came to call the Old Testament. Yes, it is part of Christian Bibles, but in Christian oversimplification, following Paul, the laws it contains are "letter" rather than "spirit" (see Romans 2:25–29; 2 Corinthians 3:6). Paul's views were not immediately accepted, however, as opposing views also found in the New Testament make clear. In the Sermon on the Mount, referring to the Jewish scriptures, Jesus is reported to have said:

> Do not think that I have come to abolish the Law and
> the Prophets: I have not come to abolish but to fulfill.
> Amen I say to you, until heaven and earth pass away,
> not one iota or one stroke will pass away from the Law,
> until everything has taken place. So whoever annuls
> one of the least of these commandments and teaches
> people to do so will be called least in the kingdom
> of heaven. But whoever does and teaches them will
> be called great in the kingdom of heaven. (Matthew
> 5:17–19)[11]

Paul, of course, was someone teaching exactly that, that the Law—the Torah—was irrelevant for Gentile Christians, so in the words the gospel of Matthew attributes to Jesus we overhear the other side of the debate, with a thinly veiled attack on Paul and his partisans.

Another expression of the view that the Torah continued to be binding on all Christians, Gentiles as well as Jews, is the letter of James. This is often attributed to Jesus's brother James,[12] who, at least according to Paul, was the leader of the "circumcision faction," opposing Paul's views about Gentiles not having to fully observe the laws of the Torah (see Galatians 2:12). According to several nonbiblical sources, James died, or was killed, in the 60s, and if the letter was in fact written by him, then he was a contemporary of Paul. On the other hand, the letter is written in excellent Greek, which seems unlikely for Jesus's brother, so other scholars conclude that it is pseudonymous, and probably to be dated to the 80s or 90s. In either case, it is a very Jewish-sounding text, apart from two explicit mentions of Jesus Christ (James 1:1; 2:1).

The author of the letter of James wrote:

> You do well if you truly fulfill the royal law according to the scripture, "You should love your neighbor as yourself." But if you show favoritism, then you have committed sin, and are guilty as transgressors under the law. Whoever keeps the whole law but falls short in one detail has become guilty of breaking all of it. For the one who said "Do not commit adultery" also said "Do not murder." If you do not commit adultery but murder, you have become a transgressor of the law. (James 2:8–11)

Like other first-century CE Jewish and Christian writers, the author of the letter of James thought that the essence of the

Law was love of neighbor, especially the most vulnerable.[13] But his language about failing in one detail sounds very similar to Matthew's.

It is even clearer that the author of the letter of James is arguing against Paul in his choice of language and proof texts from scripture, especially with regard to Abraham. Paul had written:

> What then shall we say was gained by Abraham, our ancestor according to the flesh? For if Abraham was justified by works, he has something to boast about, but not before God. For what does the scripture say? "Abraham had faith in God and it was credited to him as justification." . . . How then was it credited to him? When he was circumcised, or when he still had a foreskin? Not when he was circumcised, but while he still had a foreskin. For he received the sign of circumcision as a seal of the justification of faith while he still had a foreskin. (Romans 4:1–3, 10–11; the quotation is from Genesis 15:6)

In Paul's rabbinic-like logic, according to Genesis Abraham was justified because of his faith, before he was circumcised: the divine command to be circumcised is given and carried out in Genesis 17, two chapters after Abraham has been deemed righteous. Therefore circumcision, and by extension other works of the law, are not necessary for justification. Using the same vocabulary, the author of the letter of James disagrees:

> Do you want to know, you empty person, that faith without works is fruitless? Was not our father

Abraham justified by works when he offered his son
Isaac on the altar? You see that faith was at work along
with his works, and by his works his faith was made
complete, and the scripture was fulfilled that says,
"Abraham had faith in God, and it was credited to
him as justification." You see that a man is justified by
works, and not by faith alone. (James 2:20–24)

Someone, then, either Jesus's brother James himself or
someone using his name, was directly refuting Paul. Both
the letter of James and parts of the gospel of Matthew attest
to an ongoing debate in early Christianity between Jewish Christians and Paul about the status of the Torah, both
during Paul's life and for some time after his death, which occurred in the 60s. The terms of the debate morphed into the
slogans of the Reformation: "justification by faith," letter"
as opposed to "spirit," and "faith without works" — slogans
that had little to do with their original context. So convinced
was Martin Luther that the indulgences promoted for profit
by the Roman hierarchy — their "works" — were unneces-
sary that he called the letter of James a "strawy epistle," not
written by James the brother of Jesus, and moved it from its
usual position in the New Testament to the very end, after the
books he deemed more theologically correct — that is, more in
agreement with his views.

Eventually, Paul's position won the day, partly because
Gentile Christians soon outnumbered Jewish Christians, and
also because Jewish Christianity, headquartered in Jerusalem,
was considerably weakened by the city's destruction by the

Romans in 70 CE and by the Romans' defeat of the Second Jewish Revolt in 135. Christians were no longer obliged to obey all of the commandments of the Torah, especially those having to do with circumcision and diet. Only the Decalogue continued to be binding, and not so much because it was in the Torah, but because it was considered a natural law given by God to all. So Christians, following good Jewish practice, privileged the Decalogue, but in the process downgraded other laws in the rest of the Torah in which it is embedded. Those laws were "established by angels, through the hand of a mediator" (Galatians 3:19);[14] they are therefore inferior because, as Jewish thinkers had observed, God did not give them to the Israelites directly. As such, they were not as binding as the Decalogue, which came directly from God long before Sinai. So, at least for Gentile Christians, the requirements of the Torah were annulled.

In response to this Christian insistence that of all the laws given on Sinai, only the Decalogue was binding, because it was universal, Jewish practice changed. The Decalogue was no longer included in the texts of phylacteries and mezuzahs or in texts recited at worship, and rabbinic authorities explained why: "Because of the claims of the heretics, so that they should not say, 'Only these were given to him, to Moses, at Sinai'" (*Mishnah Berakot* 1:3). The precise identity of the "heretics" (Hebrew *minim*) is debated, but it is likely that among them were Christians. Later Jewish scholars would count some 613 commandments in the Torah (including the Ten Commandments in the total); all are equally binding, because they come from God, whether directly, or indirectly through Moses.[15] Both Jews and Christians, then, adopted extreme positions to counter each other's claims, positions inconsistent with the scriptures that they both claimed to be authoritative.

7

UP FOR GRABS?
THE SELECTIVE
OBSERVANCE OF THE
TEN COMMANDMENTS

When asked about Catholics who feel alienated from
the church because of disagreements over social issues,
such as gay marriage, [Cardinal] O'Malley replied,
"The Ten Commandments are not up for grabs."
—*The Boston Globe*, March 10, 2011

LIKE MANY OTHER SEXUAL MATTERS, GAY MARRIAGE IS
not mentioned in the Ten Commandments, so supporting
same-sex relationships is not in any way a violation of the
Decalogue, although it is admittedly contrary to older biblical laws whose modern applicability I think questionable. But
I will stick with the Decalogue for now. The assertion of Sean
Cardinal O'Malley, Roman Catholic archbishop of Boston,
assumes that the Ten Commandments are immutable, presumably because they were divinely given.

Careful reading of the Bible shows otherwise. As we
have seen, the text of the Ten Commandments was not fixed

in ancient Israel: the Bible preserves three versions, two of which are close but not identical, and one of which is very different. The existence of these three versions is important for our estimation of the Decalogue's authority. Although the biblical writers did cloak the three Decalogues with the myth of divine authorship, as is the case for the rest of the Bible we can scarcely credit the deity with such inconsistency and repetition. Instead of an allegedly divinely revealed set of universal moral codes, we have variants of historically conditioned texts, none of which in their present form go back directly to Moses, let alone to God. If there was a proto-Decalogue, as it were, it is no longer recoverable. Nor did this seem to matter to the biblical writers, for whom the actual words of the Decalogue were not as important as its underlying principles: love of God and love of neighbor.

We find a similar flexibility with regard to the wording of the Decalogue in modern times. We have already considered the abridged and watered-down version of the Ten Commandments in Exodus 20 promulgated by the Fraternal Order of Eagles.[1] The same is true of the version that I memorized as a child in parochial school from the *Baltimore Catechism*, the standard religious education textbook for American Catholics from the late nineteenth to the mid-twentieth centuries:

The commandments of God are these ten:

1. I am the Lord thy God; thou shalt not have strange gods before Me.[2]

2. Thou shalt not take the name of the Lord thy God in vain.

3. Remember thou keep holy the Lord's day.

4. Honor thy father and thy mother.

5. Thou shalt not kill.

6. Thou shalt not commit adultery.

7. Thou shalt not steal.

8. Thou shalt not bear false witness against thy neighbor.

9. Thou shalt not covet thy neighbor's wife.

10. Thou shalt not covet thy neighbor's goods.[3]

This version is closer to the one found in Deuteronomy 5 than it is to the one in Exodus 19. But we do find notable changes. The commandment about graven images has simply been omitted: what would Catholic children—and adults—think about that prohibition when they stepped inside their churches and gazed at the statues and stained glass windows? "Sabbath" has been gratuitously altered to "the Lord's day," perhaps to forestall awkward questions about which day of the week actually was the Sabbath. Like the Fraternal Order of Eagles' version, this one also leaves out the historical reference to the Exodus from Egypt, along with the problematic notions of God's punishment of generations for their ancestors' sins and the creation of the world in six days. Finally, in the *Baltimore Catechism* version, not only is the reference to slavery in the Sabbath commandment omitted, but the list of property (here the tenth commandment) is shortened from house, slaves, and livestock simply to "goods," again conveniently removing the reference to slavery.[4]

Both abridgments serve to transform the Decalogue from a particular address in a particular historical context to particular Israelites by a particular deity, Yahweh, to something more generic. At least the actual words of the Decalogue, then, have been "up for grabs" since biblical times.

So too has been some of its substance. As we have seen, Christians have not observed the commandment to rest on the seventh day literally. Most, but not all, Christians have cavalierly changed the day of rest from Saturday to Sunday, without biblical warrant. A similar lack of observance concerns images. In ancient Israel, the commandment prohibiting making images was repeatedly ignored, and even broken, and not all of these failures in observance were judged reprehensible. Moses is not condemned for making the bronze serpent, which according to the narrative he did at divine command, nor for the construction of the elaborate cherubim throne of Yahweh, which again according to the narrative God himself had ordered and whose exact specifications he had given. Solomon is not condemned for the many other cherubim and oxen and lions that adorned his Temple and palace, most of which are also found in the restoration of the Temple revealed to the prophet Ezekiel (compare 1 Kings 6–7 and Ezekiel 40–41). Yet for some biblical writers, like the scrupulous Deuteronomists, the aniconic commandment was unambiguous: the sacred space was to be unadorned with cherubim and other creatures.

Disregard of the prohibition of graven images continued in Jewish and Christian history. A stunning mosaic floor in the apse of a sixth-century CE synagogue at Beth Alpha in southern Galilee provides one example. In the top panel is a representation of a Torah shrine flanked by menorahs, birds, and lions. In the bottom panel is a charmingly naïve depiction of the near-sacrifice of Isaac. The large middle panel (Figure 6) is the most surprising, featuring the sun god in his

FIGURE 6. Detail of mosaic from the Beth Alpha synagogue. Photo credit: Art Resource, NY.

chariot drawn by four horses, encircled by the twelve signs of the zodiac, whose names are written in Hebrew. In the corners of the middle panel are the four seasons, depicted as winged goddesses. Such exuberant representational Jewish art is characteristic of the Byzantine period; we find another example, a few centuries earlier, at Dura Europos in eastern Syria, whose synagogue has several frescoes of biblical scenes.

Not far from the synagogue in cosmopolitan, pluralistic Dura Europos was a Mithraeum, a shrine dedicated to the originally Persian deity Mithra, whose "mysteries" were extremely popular throughout the Roman Empire, and an early Christian church, whose frescoes show scenes from the Gospels. Other Christian examples are too numerous to catalogue. Let us just glance at one example, the acme of Renaissance religious art, the Sistine Chapel in the Vatican, where frescoes by Michelangelo and other artists depict biblical scenes and characters. In the center of the ceiling is a series of scenes illustrating the first eleven chapters of Genesis, in which a very anthropomorphic deity is repeatedly depicted (Figure 7).

My point is obvious: neither in ancient Israel nor in subsequent Judaism and Christianity was the commandment prohibiting images consistently observed. Their use has been rationalized by the argument that they are not false gods who are worshipped, but images of the one true God, or of angels and saints who are not actually worshipped, but only "venerated." But this is a self-serving interpretation of the prohibition, which iconoclasts from biblical to modern times

FIGURE 7. Michelangelo's depiction of the creation of Adam on the ceiling of the Sistine Chapel. Sistine Chapel Ceiling (1508–12): *The Creation of Adam*, 1511–12 (fresco) (post restoration), Buonarroti, Michelangelo (1475–1564) / Vatican Museums and Galleries, Vatican City / The Bridgeman Art Library.

have strenuously insisted should be obeyed literally. The avoidance of images of Yahweh in particular in ancient Israel clearly shows that the aniconic view was the primary meaning of the commandment.

Related to the issue of graven images is that of the worship of other gods, expressly prohibited in the first commandment. As we have seen, for much of their history the ancient Israelites were not monotheists in an absolute sense. When strict monotheism began to be articulated relatively late in the biblical period, some surprising developments occurred. In polytheism, such phenomena as disease, natural disasters, and even defeat by an enemy can be attributed to malevolent deities who are always at war with the beneficent deities: sometimes one group has the upper hand, sometimes the other. But monotheism has no such simple explanation for what is often called the problem of evil. How can a loving, just, and all-powerful God allow, or even cause, the good, the righteous, and the innocent to suffer? Is there divine justice, theodicy, in the world? If there is only one god, and he (or she) is by definition supremely good, then how can he (or she) be responsible for evil? But if God is not responsible for evil, then he (or she) is not all-powerful. Conversely, if God is responsible for evil, then he (or she) is clearly not good and loving. As Archibald MacLeish put it in *J.B.*, his dramatic modernization of the book of Job:

> I heard upon his dry dung heap
> That man cry out who cannot sleep:
> "If God is God He is not good,
> If God is good, he is not God;
> Take the even, take the odd,
> I would not sleep here if I could."[5]

Biblical writers wrestled with this problem and came to no clear conclusion. For the authors of the books of Job and Ecclesiastes, divine justice was mysterious, even incomprehensible. For them both, moreover, the issue was located only in this life; there was no meaningful life after death. As time went on, however, some groups in Judaism, followed by Christianity and Islam, attempted to resolve the apparent inconsistency that God does not always reward the good and punish the wicked by developing increasingly elaborate conceptions of life after death. Then God's justice will finally be manifest: the good rewarded in heaven, the wicked punished according to their deserts in different levels of hell, and, in Christian doctrine, those neither saintly nor hopelessly sinful with terms in purgatory.

Another attempt to solve the problem of evil was to return to a kind of polytheism. God was not the only power at work in the cosmos. He was opposed by an evil force—named Satan, Mastema, the devil, Iblis, and so on—who was responsible for sin, suffering, and disease. In a way, this lets God off the hook, but not entirely: if God is all-powerful, why can he not control this adversary, and if he can, then is he not in the end ultimately responsible for everything that does or does not happen to the good and the bad? Satan, to be sure, has not been worshipped by mainstream monotheists. Moreover, Satan is not the only power other than God at work in the cosmos.

There are legions of other semi-divine, even divine beings: devils and demons, angels with their many ranks, saints already in heaven, and most interestingly, female associates of God. In Judaism, there is the Shekinah, the personified and quasi-deified divine presence, the "bride of the Sabbath"; in Christianity there is especially Mary, the mother of Jesus; and in Islam, the three goddesses of the "Satanic verses," al-Lat, al-Uzza, and Manat (*Qur'an* 53.19–20). These female beings complement the male patriarchal God of monotheism. In Roman Catholic and Eastern Orthodox Christianity, in fact,

Mary is functionally a goddess. She is popularly believed to be very powerful—"If God won't listen to you, he will listen to his mother!" She is the queen of heaven, and with her son, co-redemptrix—co-savior—of the world, beliefs that have no scriptural basis. Before her statue people light candles, place flowers, kneel, and pray. When such actions occur in other religions, we call it worship, and I would argue that that is what it is with regard to Mary, despite the fine distinctions theologians make between "veneration" and "worship." It is not a great leap from Mariolatry to idolatry, as many Christians, along with Jews and Muslims, have observed.[6]

In Christianity we also find the Trinity. For Jews and Muslims (and Unitarians), Christian belief in the divinity of Jesus and three persons in one God is not monotheistic, no matter how Christian theologians have parsed it. The Qur'an is emphatic: "The Messiah, Jesus, son of Mary, was only the Messenger of God. . . . So believe in God and His Messengers, and say not, 'Three'" (4.171).[7] The alternate understanding of the opening words of the Shema implies the same—"The LORD our God, the LORD is one." It may be a matter of interpretation, but from the perspective of the other two monotheistic religions, Christianity's claim to be monotheistic is questionable.

Issues of images and polytheism aside, there are also values enshrined in the Decalogue that most Jews and Christians have for good reasons abandoned in modern times. The first is slavery, now universally rejected. Both the Sabbath commandment and the tenth commandment mention slaves. I would think that if these were originally from a deity who freed the Hebrew slaves from Egyptian bondage, he might at least hint that slavery was intrinsically wrong. But we find no such hint. Slaves are to be provided rest on the Sabbath, and Deuteronomy's expansion of the Sabbath commandment tells us why: the Israelites know what it is like to be slaves; still, their own slaves are only to be given rest, not freed. And, as the last commandment makes clear, they are property.

In the laws that follow the Decalogue in the book of Exodus, slavery is an established institution, regulated by divinely given legislation. Slaves belonged to their owners, either for a term, when paying off a debt, or for life. Here is one law that shows the difference between a slave and a free person:

> When a man strikes the eye of his male slave or the eye of his female slave, and destroys it, he should let him go free to compensate for his eye. And if he knocks out the tooth of his male slave or the tooth of his female slave, he should let him go free to compensate for his tooth. (Exodus 21:26–27)

This law immediately follows the "eye for eye, tooth for tooth" formula, but that principle does not apply to slaves, who were a lesser class, in Israel as in the rest of the ancient Near East. Because of the harm the violent owner caused, he is to be punished, but only financially: he loses his slave, but not his eye or his tooth. Because of biblical warrant, like Jews Christians would continue to be slave owners for many centuries, for nowhere in the New Testament is slavery condemned.

Slaves were not the only persons considered property; women were as well. Note this law, which combines the two:

> When a man sells his daughter as a female slave, she will not go out as male slaves do. If she is bad in the eyes of her lord, who had designated her for himself, then he should let her be bought back. He is not authorized to sell her to a foreign people, because he has been unfair to her. If he designates her for his son, he should treat her as is customary with daughters. If he takes another woman for himself, he may not diminish her food, her clothing, or her conjugal rights. And if he does not provide her with these three things, then she may go out without compensation or payment of silver. (Exodus 21:7–11)

Why would a father sell his daughter? Because he needed the money! Male debtors could be enslaved for no more than seven years, but for the daughter there is no such term limit. She has simply been sold by her father to someone else, who now has control over her; he can even give her to his son as a wife or concubine. There are restrictions: she may not be resold, at least not to a non-Israelite; she may be returned for a refund if the buyer finds her unsatisfactory; and if the buyer treats her unfairly, she may simply leave without penalty. But despite these restrictions, a man's daughter is clearly able to be sold into slavery, for she is his property.

This illustrates the subordinate status of women in biblical times, a status not much better than that of slaves. A woman was the property of the man who controlled her—

her father or her husband. This status underlies the last commandment, which lists a man's property: house, wife, slaves, livestock. In Deuteronomy's version, the order is slightly changed—wife, real estate, slaves, livestock—but that does not alter the woman's status. This value too, although enshrined in the Decalogue, is one that most Jews and Christians—but only in the past century or so—have rejected, in principle if not entirely in practice.

Some of these issues are relatively trivial, others less so. But taken cumulatively, they illustrate that from biblical times to the present, different writers and religious authorities, at various times and places, have expanded, revised, and amended the Decalogue, and even disregarded some of its explicit commands and implicit values, even though it was supposedly from God, or Moses, or both.

We no longer have the original tablets on which the Ten Commandments were supposedly written. In my view, we should not re-create and then display them, according to what we might like them to have been. Moreover, the first four commandments especially should not be implicitly imposed on our pluralistic society.[8] Neither my atheist nor my Hindu neighbors should be required or even urged to worship the god of Israel, or only him. Many modern churches and some synagogues feature representations of figures from biblical history and even of God himself, and graven images of our national heroes hold sway in our parks. Use of words like "so help me God" in court or in oaths of new citizens, in inauguration ceremonies, and in courts of law is often no longer required. Even Sabbath observance has dramatically diminished in American custom, partly because different days of rest are observed (or not) by different groups, and also because, I suppose, commerce often trumps religion. The last six commandments, to be sure, in their essence articulate a principle necessary for any society to function: a person's life, marriage, reputation, and property are inviolable under most circumstances. They should be followed for that reason, not because they happen to be found in the Bible.

8

HONORING THE
TEN COMMANDMENTS

INSIDE THE SUPREME COURT BUILDING IN WASHINGTON, D.C., friezes on the north and south walls of the court chamber depict great lawgivers of history in chronological order. The ensemble is remarkably ecumenical and international. From the ancient Near East we see Menes, Hammurapi, Moses, and Solomon (Figure 8). From the Far East we see Confucius. Ancient Greece and Rome are represented by Lycurgus, Solon, Draco, Octavian, and Justinian. We also see Muhammad, and finally a cluster of Europeans — King John of England, King Louis IX of France, the Dutch jurist Hugo Grotius, the British legal theorist William Blackstone, and Napoleon — among whom is the American jurist John Marshall. All the figures are the same size, with none presented as more important than the others.

Moses is holding two tablets, but only the edge of the first is visible behind the second. On the second are written the last five commandments, in Hebrew, beginning with "You should not murder." The choice of these, rather than all ten, as elsewhere in the Supreme Court building, is

FIGURE 8. Part of the south wall frieze inside the Supreme Court, showing, from left, the personified figure of Fame; Menes, the first king of Egypt; Hammurapi, the king of Babylon who promulgated his Code; Moses; Authority; and Solomon. Photo credit: Collection of the Supreme Court of the United States.

instructive. Here, in a parade of famous lawgivers, Moses is shown as giving essentially secular commandments, prohibiting murder, adultery, kidnapping, perjury, and theft, principles necessary for any functioning society. Not shown are the first five commandments, the first four of which are distinctively Israelite, having to do with the worship of Yahweh and with the Sabbath. Adolph Weinman, the sculptor of the frieze, deliberately, and appropriately, hid the religious content of the Decalogue. It is part of the history of law, but it is not specially privileged. Moses is the lawgiver, not God, even though, as is also the case with other notables depicted on the frieze, including Hammurapi and Muhammad, the laws that he promulgated were believed to have a divine origin.

We also find Moses and the Ten Commandments elsewhere in the Supreme Court building. The exterior east pediment features three lawgivers, in the midst of allegorical figures. Moses, holding one tablet with each hand, is in the center, flanked by the smaller figures of Confucius and Solon (Figure 9). In this group, Moses is clearly privileged by his size and his position. Yet, remarkably, the tablets are blank. The sculptor, Hermon MacNeil, did not call attention to the actual content of the Decalogue, either its religious or its secular requirements, nor to the divine origin of the laws: again, Moses, not God, is the lawgiver.

Two other depictions of the Ten Commandments, on doors leading into the chamber and on metal gates at the east façade, show only the tablets, with roman numerals on them but no text; God is not speaking, except implicitly. (Roman

FIGURE 9. From left to right, Confucius, Moses, and Solon, on the east side of the Supreme Court Building in Washington, D.C. Photo credit: Collection of the Supreme Court of the United States.

numerals are often anachronistically used for the Ten Commandments, presumably because they give a vaguely ancient look.) For the designers of the Supreme Court building, at least, if not for all the justices who sit on the bench, the Decalogue has been stripped of its explicit religious content. They are, in other words, part of the history of law, but are not primarily religious texts, inspired scripture. Moreover, unlike art we might find in some houses of worship, nowhere in the Supreme Court is God depicted giving the tablets to Moses. (I cannot resist noting that the sculptures themselves are prima facie evidence for violation of the commandment prohibiting the making of images.)

In *Van Orden v. Perry*, the justices of the plurality opinion upholding the constitutionality of the Ten Commandments monument on the grounds of the state capitol in Austin noted the multiple displays of the Decalogue in their building.[1] But the Texas monument, and others like it, is very different (see Figure 2), with many explicitly religious symbols and, more or less, the text of the supposedly divinely given commandments.

In my view, the frieze in the court chamber of the Supreme Court provides a model for how to publicly recognize the importance of the Ten Commandments in an American context. They are certainly part of our history, and of world history. But like the interpretation and the observance of the Decalogue, that history has not been static. We are a very different country now than we were in the late eighteenth century, or in 1935 when the Supreme Court building was completed. We are much more diverse, especially religiously; we should not, we may not elevate a text from one or two religious traditions to a privileged status. In the American system, the commandments detailing obligations to God must be left to individual believers and their faith communities. The remaining commandments, having to do with honoring parents and protecting from murder, adultery, kidnapping, perjury, and expropriation of property, are essentially secular and are found in most legal systems.

As we have seen, the Ten Commandments are no longer set in stone, if they ever were. The Bible has not just one version of the Ten Commandments, but at least three, different in many small details and in larger ways as well. These variants show that the Ten Commandments could not have been divinely given. Furthermore, the human writers of the Bible disagreed with each other, sometimes radically. The principle of transgenerational punishment enshrined in the third commandment is emphatically rejected by the prophet Ezekiel, and Jesus rejected some of the supposedly divinely proclaimed dictates of biblical law. With its various versions and interpretations of the Decalogue, the Bible both forces us and even authorizes us to continue to do the same—to reformulate, to interpret, even to ignore and to reject. In fact, that is precisely what Jews and Christians have done, from biblical times to the present, because the values of the biblical writers are in many respects no longer ours. But on questions of values, in the present as in the past, there is seldom full agreement.

The continuing arguments about display of the Ten Commandments are not about the Ten Commandments themselves, and certainly not in any secular sense. The arguments are, patently, an expression of one side in the ongoing culture war that divides the United States, and much of the world, a war about ultimate human values. Defenders of the display of the Decalogue assert, or at least imply, that we have infallible answers in an ancient text to complex modern questions. They interpret that text inflexibly, which is at odds with the text itself, as well as with the history of its (non)observance. Public display of the Decalogue—making it a graven image, as it were—is also unhistorical. It suggests that it is an immutable text, written in stone, but for Jews and Christians over the ages it has not always been so.

It is deeply ironic that those supporting the display of the Ten Commandments defend it by claiming that they are doing so only because of the secular, historical importance of the Decalogue. For them, clearly, the text is indisputably a sacred text, not at all equivalent to the Code of Hammurapi or the Napoleonic Code or Sharia derived from the Qur'an. In fact, display of the Ten Commandments is a blatant and unAmerican effort to impose a basically Christian perspective on all citizens of the United States. The version of the Ten Commandments that is displayed—and often its accompanying symbols—does not correspond to any actual biblical text of the Decalogue, but it is closest to the one followed by most Protestants. So it leaves out not only the religiously unaffiliated and atheists, but Hindus, Buddhists, Sikhs, Muslims, and the other religions that enrich American culture, and even Jews and other Christians.

Finally, I would argue that display of the Ten Commandments is not only un-American, but contrary to the underlying values of the Bible. Those values are what matter, not the actual words, with their historically conditioned contents and in their multiple versions. According to the Torah, among the laws God gave to Moses was this: "You should love your neighbor as yourself" (Leviticus 19:18). About this law, agreeing with Hillel, Jesus, and Paul, the late first/early second-century CE Rabbi Akiba said: "'You should love your neighbor as yourself' is the greatest principle in the Torah" (*Sifra* 89b).[2] That ethos has informed our society's best instincts, freeing slaves, empowering women, welcoming immigrants, caring for the poor and powerless, and considering all persons as equal. It can also continue to inform us, as we strive to love all of our neighbors, as they are, here in the United States and in the global community to which we belong, regardless of their age, gender, sexual orientation, ethnicity, national origin, social status, and religious beliefs or lack of them. That is how to honor the Ten Commandments.

AN ANCIENT TREATY

Here are excerpts of a treaty between Mursili II, the king of Hatti (the Hittites), in Asia Minor and his vassal, Tuppi-Teshub, the king of Amurru, in northern Lebanon. It dates to the late fourteenth century BCE. Translation by Gary A. Beckman, *Hittite Diplomatic Texts* (Atlanta, GA: Scholars Press, 2nd ed., 1999), 59–64.

IDENTIFICATION OF THE SUZERAIN

Thus says My Majesty, Mursili, Great King, King of Hatti, Hero, Beloved of the Storm God, son of Suppiluliuma, Great King, King of Hatti, Hero:

HISTORICAL SUMMARY OF THE SUZERAIN'S RELATIONSHIP TO THE VASSAL

Aziru, your grandfather, Tuppi-Teshub, became the subject of my father. When it came about that the kings of the land of Nuhashshi and the king of the land of Kinza became hostile to my father, Aziru did not become hostile. When my father made war on his enemies, Aziru likewise made war. And Aziru protected only my father, and my father protected Aziru, together with his land. He did not seek to harm him in any way. And Aziru did not anger my father in any way. He always paid him the 300 shekels of refined, first-class gold which he had imposed as tribute. My father died, and I took my seat upon the throne of my father. But as Aziru had been in the time of my father, so he was in my time. . . .

But when your father died, according to the request of your father, I did not cast you off. Because your father had spoken your name before me during his lifetime, I therefore took care of you. But you were sick and ailing. And although you were an invalid, I nonetheless installed you in place of your father. I made your brothers and the land of Amurru swear an oath to you.

OBLIGATIONS OF THE SUZERAIN TO THE VASSAL AND OF THE VASSAL TO THE SUZERAIN

And as I took care of you according to the request of your father, and installed you in place of your father, I have now made you swear an oath to the King of Hatti and the land of Hatti, and to my sons and grandsons. Observe the oath and the authority of the King. I, My Majesty, will protect you, Tuppi-Teshub. And when you take a wife and produce a son, he shall later be king in the land of Amurru. And as you protect My Majesty, I will likewise protect your son. You, Tuppi-Teshub, in the future protect the King of Hatti, the land of Hatti, my sons, and my grandsons. The tribute which was imposed upon your grandfather and upon your father shall be imposed upon you. . . .

Whoever is My Majesty's enemy shall be your enemy. Whoever is My Majesty's friend shall be your friend. And if any of the lands which are protectorates of the King of Hatti should become hostile to the King of Hatti, and if I, My Majesty, come against that land for attack, and you do not mobilize wholeheartedly with infantry and chariotry, and do not make war wholeheartedly and without hesitation on the enemy, you will transgress the oath. . . .

As I, My Majesty, protect you, Tuppi-Teshub, be an auxiliary army for My Majesty and for Hatti. And if some evil matter arises in Hatti and someone revolts against My Majesty, and you hear of it, lend assistance together with your infantry and your chariotry. Take a stand immediately to help Hatti. But if it is not possible for you to lend assistance personally, send aid to the King of Hatti by either your son or your brother, together with your infantry and your chariotry. If you do not send aid to the king of Hatti by your son or your brother, together with your infantry and your chariotry, you will transgress the oath.

If some matter oppresses you, Tuppi-Teshub, or someone revolts against you, and you write to the King of Hatti, then the King of Hatti will send infantry and chariotry to your aid.

If Hittites bring you, Tuppi-Teshub, infantry and chariotry—because they will go up to your cities, Tuppi-Teshub must regularly provide them with food and drink. And if any

Hittite undertakes an evil matter against Tuppi-Teshub, such as the plunder of his land or of his cities, or the removal of Tuppi-Teshub from kingship in the land of Amurru, he will transgress the oath.

Whatever civilian captives of the land of Nuhashshi and the land of Kinza my father carried off, or I carried off—if one of these civilian captives flees from me and comes to you, and you do not seize him and give him back to the King of Hatti, you will transgress the oath. And if you should even think as follows concerning a fugitive: "Come or go! Wherever you go, I don't want to know about you."—you will transgress the oath....

If someone should bring up before you, Tuppi-Teshub, evil matters against the King or against Hatti, you shall not conceal him from the King. Or if My Majesty speaks confidentially of some matters to you: "Perform these deeds or that deed," then make an appeal right there at that moment concerning whatever among those deeds you do not want to perform: "I cannot do this deed. I will not perform it." And when the King again commands, and you do not perform a deed of which you are capable, but rebuff the King, or if you do not observe the matter of which the King speaks to you confidentially, you will transgress the oath.

If some population or fugitive sets out, travels toward Hatti, and passes through your land, set them well on their way and point out the road to Hatti. Speak favorable words to them. You shall not direct them to anyone else. If you do not set them on their way and do not show them the road to

Hatti, but direct them to the mountains—or if you speak evil words before them, you will transgress the oath.

Or if the King of Hatti beleaguers some country through battle, and it flees before him, and comes into your country— if you want to take anything, ask the King of Hatti for it. You shall not take it on your own initiative. If you take anything on your own initiative and conceal it, you will transgress the oath....

INVOCATION OF DIVINE WITNESSES

The Thousand Gods shall now stand for this oath. They shall observe and listen. The Sun God of Heaven, the Sun Goddess of Arinna, the Storm God of Heaven, the Storm God of Hatti, Sheri, Hurri, Mount Nanni, Mount Hazzi, the Storm God of the Market, the Storm God of the Army, the Storm God of Aleppo, the Storm God of Zippalanda, the Storm God of Nerik, the Storm God of Lihzina, the Storm God of the Ruin Mound, the Storm God of Hisashapa, the Storm God of Sahpina, the Storm God of Sapinuwa, the Storm God of Pittiyarik, the Storm God of Šamuha, the Storm God of Hurma, the Storm God of Sarissa, the Storm God of Help, the Storm God of Uda, the Storm God of Kizzuwatna, the Storm God of Ishupitta, the Storm God of ..., the Storm God of Arkata, the Storm God of Tunip, the Storm God of Aleppo resident in Tunip, Milku of the land of Amurru, the Tutelary Deity, the Tutelary Deity of Hatti, Zithariya, Karzi, Hapantaliya, the Tutelary Deity of Karahna, the Tutelary Deity of the Countryside, the Tutelary Deity of the Hunting Bag, Ea, Allatu, Telipinu of Turmitta, Telipinu of Tawaniya, Telipinu of Hanhana, Bunene, Askasepa, the Moon God, Lord of the Oath, Ishara, Queen of the Oath, Hebat, Queen of Heaven, Ishtar, Ishtar of the Countryside, Ishtar of Nineveh, Ishtar of Hattarina, Ninatta, Kulitta, the War God of Hatti, the War God of Illaya, the War God of Arziya, Yarri, Zappana, Hantitassu of Hurma, Abara of Samuha, Katahha of Ankuwa, the Queen of Katapa, Ammamma of Tahurpa, Hallara of Dunna, Huwassanna of Hupisna, Tapisuwa of Ishupitta, the Lady of Landa, Kuniyawanni of Landa, NIN.PISAN.PISAN of Kinza, Mount Lebanon, Mount Shariyana, Mount Pishaisha, the mountain-dweller gods, the mercenary gods, Ereshkigal, the male deities and female deities of Hatti, the male deities and female deities of Amurru, all the primeval deities—Mara, Namsara, Minki, Tuhusi, Ammunki, Ammizzadu, Alalu, Antu, Anu, Apantu, Enlil, Ninlil—the mountains, the rivers, the springs, the great sea, heaven and earth, the winds, the clouds. They shall be witnesses to this treaty and to the oath.

CURSES AND BLESSINGS

All the words of the treaty and oath which are written on this tablet—if Tuppi-Teshub does not observe these words of the treaty and of the oath, then these oath gods shall destroy Tuppi-Teshub, together with his person, his wife, his son, his grandsons, his household, his city, his land, and together with his possessions.

But if Tuppi-Teshub observes these words of the treaty and of the oath which are written on this tablet, then these oath gods shall protect Tuppi-Teshub, together with his person, his wife, his son, his grandsons, his city, his land, his household, his subjects, and together with his possessions.

NOTES

Following current scholarly practice, I use the abbreviations BCE (Before the Common Era) and CE (Common Era) for the older BC and AD. I also sometimes use "Hebrew Bible" to refer to the canonical Bible of Judaism, in preference to the more explicitly Christian "Old Testament."

Chapter and verse numbers occasionally vary in different Bibles. Here I follow those used in the New Revised Standard Version, which at times are slightly different from those in the New Jewish Publication Society translation (Tanakh) and from those in older Roman Catholic and Orthodox Bibles.

Unless otherwise indicated, all translations of ancient texts are my own.

1 IDOLS AND IMAGES

1. The Fraternal Order of Eagles is responsible for a large number — probably several hundred — of these monuments.

2. Also on the basis of its longevity, the very commercial CITGO sign in Boston has become an unofficial landmark.

2. A CONTRACT SEALED WITH BLOOD

1. Most biblical sources place Mount Sinai east of the Red Sea in southern Jordan or northern Saudi Arabia. The traditional identification of Jebel Musa in the southern Sinai Peninsula as Mount Sinai has no geographical or archaeological basis; the name was first attached to this impressive peak by Christian pilgrims in the fourth century CE.

2. Exodus 19:1–2. In Exodus 3:1, the mountain is called Horeb; different biblical writers use different names for what was probably the same mountain.

3. The exact phrase "the ten words" is used elsewhere only in Deuteronomy 4:13 (of the first set) and 10:4 (of the replacement set). It is often translated "the ten commandments," but that is not what the Hebrew literally means.

4. In following books of the Pentateuch, God speaks not just to Moses but also, in some sources, both to Moses and his brother Aaron, to Aaron alone, and to a few chosen others.

5. *b. Makkot* 24a; *b. Horayot* 8a. I owe this reference to Moshe Weinfeld, *Deuteronomy 1–11* (Anchor Bible 5; New York: Doubleday, 1964), 240.

6. See Gad B. Sarfatti, "The Tablets of the Law as a Symbol of Judaism," in *The Ten Commandments in History and Tradition* (ed. Ben-Zion Segal and Gershon Levi; Jerusalem: The Magnes Press of the Hebrew University of Jerusalem, 1990), 407–17.

7. In other biblical traditions, the entire text of the law — "the teaching of Moses" — was also written on stone slabs that were deposited in a shrine; see Deuteronomy 27:1–8; Joshua 8:32–35.

8. The "book of the covenant" refers not to the Ten Commandments, but to the laws that follow them in Exodus 20–23.

9. For more of the text, see Michael D. Coogan, *A Reader of Ancient Near Eastern Texts: Sources for the Study of the Old Testament* (New York: Oxford University Press, 2013), 102–4. In the treaty, which is written in Aramaic, the same word for "cut" is used both for the calf in the passage above and for the treaty-making.

10. In Jewish tradition there are such supposedly universal laws, the so-called Noachian or Noahide laws, the commands given to Noah and his descendants after the biblical Flood, but not the Ten Commandments. This makes narrative sense, if not historical, since only Noah and his family survived the Flood. In Genesis 9, only two explicit prohibitions are enjoined upon Noah: not to murder, and not to consume animal blood. Later rabbis added to these other prohibitions they also considered universal, including idolatry, blasphemy, sexual immorality, and theft (the lists vary). Of the original two, only the first, prohibiting murder, remained binding in Christianity, which early in its history rejected Jewish dietary laws.

11. See Leviticus 26:3–39; Deuteronomy 27:15–26; 28; and compare Deuteronomy 11:26–28; Joshua 8:34.

3. WHICH VERSION OF THE TEN COMMANDMENTS?

1. None of the three versions of the Decalogue is numbered in the Bible itself. In this book, I follow the numbering in the middle column in Table 1 (Chapter 3).

2. The same verb and a closely related form have a sexual connotation in Genesis 39:14, 17, and probably also in Genesis 21:9; Judges 16:25; 2 Samuel 6:5, 21–22; and Proverbs 8:30–31.

3. Also found in Exodus 23:19, this may originally have been a sacrificial rubric, but in Deuteronomy 14:21 it occurs in the context of general dietary laws, which is also how it has been interpreted by Jewish tradition.

4. One of the many difficulties with this replacement set is determining exactly where the actual commandments begin; some scholars start them later than I do, with verse 12 or verse 17.

5. The Hebrew word here is usually translated "ark," but apart from its ritual use, as in the phrase "ark of the covenant," it means simply a box, like the coffin in which Joseph's mummified corpse was placed (Genesis 50:26), and the chest in which money was stored in the Temple (2 Kings 12:9–10). Differentiating themselves from the more elaborate descriptions of the ark found in what scholars call the Priestly

tradition (as in Exodus 25:10–22), the authors of Deuteronomy describe the ark as a simple wooden container in which the tablets of the law were kept (and only the tablets, according to 1 Kings 8:9); in Priestly tradition other souvenirs from the wilderness journey were also stored in it.

6. A similar inconsistency has to do with who actually wrote down the words of the Decalogue. For the first set, God himself did so; see Exodus 31:18; 32:15–16; Deuteronomy 4:13; 5:22; 9:10. But when it comes to the second set, Exodus 34:28 tells us that Moses was the writer, God's scribe, his secretary, although God was still the author. But again, I think in order to make the second set of tablets as authoritative as the first, with which for the author of Deuteronomy they are identical, he insists that God was also the writer of the second set (Deuteronomy 10:4).

4. HOW OLD ARE THE TEN COMMANDMENTS?

1. Because the dates given in the Bible for Moses and the exodus are both inconsistent and unreliable, scholars continue to disagree on the chronology. Like me, a majority, but by no means all, put them in the thirteenth century BCE, in the reign of Pharaoh Rameses II. Others, both ancient and modern, put them several centuries earlier.

2. The same phrasing is used in Deuteronomy 4:40; 5:33; 6:18; 12:25, 28; 22:7.

3. J: Exodus 34:1, 4, 28; E: Exodus 24:12; 31:18b; 32:16, 19; D: Deuteronomy 4:13; 5:19; etc.; P: Exodus 31:18a; 32:15; 34:29.

4. J: Exodus 34:28; D: Deuteronomy 4:13; 10:4.

5. Hebrew *hesed*, implying a covenant relationship, both with God and also with the neighbor. The same word is used of God in Exodus 20:6.

6. Some scholars maintain that the Jeremiah passage is later than the prophet himself; fewer would make the same claim for Hosea. In any case, whatever their exact dates, these texts further attest to both the centrality of the Decalogue and also its pervasiveness in Israelite tradition. The different order of the prohibited actions in these passages

and in the two similar versions of the Decalogue is likely due to fluidity in its formulation; note also Psalm 50:18. Similar fluidity is found in ancient translations and in later Jewish and Christian texts; see further Chapter 6.

7. See note 5 above.

8. For example, Shiloh (1 Samuel 1:7). The name "Bethel" actually means "house of God" (Genesis 28:17, 22). Other textual evidence for local shrines includes Judges 20:1 (Mizpah); Judges 20:18, 26; 21:2 (Bethel); 1 Samuel 21:1–6 (Nob); probably Hosea 9:4, and perhaps Psalms 42:4; 55:14 (in the last three texts the shrine is unnamed). This textual evidence is complemented by archaeological data of temples, mainly from the monarchic period, at sites such as Arad, Beer-sheba, and Dan.

9. To take one pertinent example, in his detailed argument for a sixth- or fifth-century BCE date for the three Decalogues (*Etched in Stone: The Emergence of the Decalogue* [New York: T & T Clark, 2006]), David H. Aaron makes no mention of what I take to be allusions to the Ten Commandments in Hosea and Jeremiah.

10. Usually mistranslated "God Almighty," El Shadday is a title of the Canaanite high god El, whom Israel's ancestors are described as worshipping, as did their contemporaries.

11. Jethro is his usual name, used in the E source, but in the J source he is called Reuel.

5. ORIGINAL MEANINGS

1. The "sons of God" are explicitly mentioned in Genesis 6:2; Deuteronomy 32:8; Psalms 29:1; 82:6; 89:6; and Job 1.6; 2:1; 38:7. Yahweh's superiority to other gods is asserted in, for example, Exodus 15:11; Psalms 71:19; 86:7; 89:6.

2. Tammuz is also the name of one of the months of the year in Hebrew.

3. Scholars have long recognized connections between a hymn to the Aten from the tomb of an Egyptian royal official and Psalm 104, but the links are almost certainly not direct.

4. One possible image of Yahweh is part of a graffito on a large store-jar from Kuntillet Ajrud, a site in the northern Sinai dating to circa 800 BCE. If it is Yahweh, as a Hebrew text (perhaps a caption) over it suggests, it is a crude depiction; his arm is linked with another figure, whom some scholars, including me, identify as Yahweh's divine wife, the goddess Asherah. But other scholars identify the figures as representations of the Egyptian god Bes. In either case, it is more representative of religious practice on the margins rather than in the capital cities.

5. The Qur'an does not specially legislate this, not does it mention the Ten Commandments explicitly. It does, however, refer repeatedly to Moses, the revelation on the mount (Sinai), and the giving of the tablets.

6. I translate the same word in Deuteronomy 5:11 as "nothing," as here, but in 5:20 as "false," for greater clarity in English; Exodus 20:7 and 20:16 use two different words.

7. The divine name Yahweh is almost certainly a form of the verb "to be," meaning perhaps "(the one who) causes (things) to be."

8. The Hebrew word translated "idols" may literally mean "balls of dung."

9. Preexilic references include 2 Kings 4:23; 16:18; Amos 8:5; Isaiah 1:13; Hosea 2:11; Jeremiah 17:20–27; Lamentations 2:6; Ezekiel 20:12–13.

10. Either a reference to debt-slavery, or to taking bribes to testify falsely against the innocent poor.

11. See also Justin, *First Apology* 67.

12. This is how Paul, or more likely others writing in his name, understood it; see Ephesians 6:1–4; Colossians 3:20.

13. See, for example, Isaiah 63:16; 64:8; Psalm 103:13; Ephesians 3:14–15.

14. See further Michael Coogan, *God and Sex: What the Bible Really Says* (New York: Twelve, 2010), 64–67.

15. See http://www.scborromeo.org/ccc/p3s2c2a6.htm.

16. See further Coogan, *God and Sex*, 101–40.

17. The Hebrew word, *ganab* (*ganav*), is the basis of Yiddish *ganef* (*gonif*), "thief."

18. Because *kleptō*, the Greek verb used to translate this Hebrew verb, has the primary meaning "steal" (compare "kleptomaniac"), when translating the word in New Testament texts I have retained the traditional rendering "steal."

19. See, for example, Deuteronomy 21:19; 22:15; Ruth 4:1–12; 1 Kings 21:8–13.

20. See, for example, 1 Samuel 3:17; 14:44; 1 Kings 2:23; 19:2; 20:10; 2 Kings 6:31.

21. Zechariah 5:3–4 makes this explicit. These verses allude to the Decalogue, pronouncing a curse both on those who kidnap (or steal) and on those who swear falsely using the divine name; see also Leviticus 19:12.

22. See also Exodus 12:49; Numbers 9:14; 15:16, 29; Ezekiel 47:22.

23. *The Commandments: Sefer Ha-Mitzvoth of Maimonides* (trans. C. B. Chavel; New York: Soncino, 1967), 2:250.

24. W. L. Lambert, *Babylonian Wisdom Literature* (Oxford: Clarendon, 1960), 232. Similar proverbs are found in other ancient texts.

6. WHICH LAWS ARE BINDING?

1. See also Josephus, *Antiquities* 3.93–94; Pseudo-Philo, *Biblical Antiquities* 11.14–15.

2. It may be significant that in Deuteronomy, the Shema (6:1–4) comes in the chapter immediately following the one in which the Decalogue is found (5;6–11).

3. See Romans 13:9 (adultery, murder, theft, desire); James 2:11 (adultery, murder); and note further Mark 7:21–22 and its variant in Matthew 15:19.

4. Love of enemies, although often considered an innovation by Jesus, is another example of Jesus's use of the Torah. Note especially Exodus 23:4 ("If you come upon your enemy's ox or his donkey straying,

you should return it to him"), and compare Deuteronomy 22:1–3, which literally refers only to "your brother's" animals.

5. *Reflections on the Psalms* (London: Geoffrey Bles, 1958), 113.

6. Compare Matthew 22:36–40; Luke 10:25–28. The opening Greek words could also be translated "Hear O Israel, the Lord our God is one lord," and the phrase "with all your mind" is not found in the original Hebrew and may be a gloss on the next, "with all your strength."

7. See Acts 18:18; 21:26; Philippians 3:5–6. Nazirites promised to lead ascetic lives, abstaining from alcohol and not cutting their hair, either forever or for a set term, after which they would offer sacrifices.

8. See further Romans 4:9–12; 5:1; 7:6.

9. Compare Deuteronomy 30:14; Jeremiah 31:33.

10. I should note that Paul disagrees about monotheism: "What is knowable about God is apparent to [the impious and the unjust]. For God made it apparent to them. . . . They exchanged the glory of the immortal God for the likeness of an image of a mortal human and of birds and four-footed animals and reptiles" (Romans 1:19, 23). For Paul, because of his Jewish background, monotheism was apparently self-evident, as was not making images.

11. Compare Luke 16:17. "The Law and the Prophets" is an inclusive term for the Jewish scriptures, whose first two parts are the Torah (the "Law") and the (Former and Latter) Prophets. The reference to "heaven and earth" may be an echo of passages like Deuteronomy 30:19 and ultimately of the divine witnesses in the Hittite treaties. The iota is the smallest letter of the Greek alphabet (like the rest of the New Testament, the gospel of Matthew was written in Greek), whose Aramaic equivalent (in the language Jesus himself certainly would have used) is *yod*; a "stroke" was the smallest part of a letter, like a serif or the crossbar on our lowercase "t."

12. See Matthew 13:55; Mark 6:3; Galatians 1:19.

13. Note especially James 1:27, which defines "pure and undefiled religion" as "caring for orphans and widows in their affliction and keeping oneself unstained by the world."

14. Compare Acts 7:53; Hebrews 2:2.

15. *b. Makkot* 23b. Rabbinic authorities disagree about the precise identification of the 613 commandments. According to the great twelfth-century scholar Maimonides, the first is in Genesis 1:28 ("Be fruitful and multiply"), and the last is in Deuteronomy 32:38 (one should not drink wine offered to other gods).

7. UP FOR GRABS?

1. Interestingly, when I went to look this up on the FOE website, I discovered that the Ten Commandments are available only on the "members only" website. Have they become an embarrassment? Certainly the group's mission now seems to be broader than dissemination of the Decalogue. A Ten Commandments monument installed on the grounds of the state capitol in Oklahoma City in 2012 was privately funded, although its design is the same as the FOE monuments.

2. In this version, based on the Catholic Douay-Rheims translation of the Bible into English from the Latin Vulgate, the word "strange" in the first commandment is simply a mistranslation of the original Hebrew.

3. See http://www.catholicity.com/baltimore-catechism/lesson15.html.

4. The FOE version, in its tenth commandment (following general Protestant numbering), has "his cattle" instead of "his ox" and "his ass," I suspect because "ass" might seem vulgar. This is similar to how the New Revised Standard Version changed the Revised Standard Version's "I will accept no bull from your house" (Psalm 50:9) to "I will not accept a bull from your house," and Paul's statement "once I was stoned" (2 Corinthians 11:25) to "once I received a stoning"; and how the revised edition of the New American Bible changed most occurrences of "booty" to words like "plunder" and "spoils."

5. *J.B.: A Play in Verse* (Boston: Houghton Mifflin, 1957), 12. These words are spoken by Nickles, the character who will assume the role of Satan.

6. See, for example, *Qur'an* 5.116: "When God said, 'O Jesus son of Mary, didst thou say unto men, "Take me and my mother as gods, apart

from God"?' He said, 'To Thee be glory! It is not mine to say what I have no right to.'" (Translated by A. J. Arberry, *The Koran Interpreted* [New York: Simon & Schuster, 1996 (1955)], 1.147.)

7. Translated by Arberry, *The Koran Interpreted*, 1.125.

8. A useful overview is provided by The Pluralism Project at Harvard University; see www.pluralism.org.

8. HONORING THE TEN COMMANDMENTS

1. The 5–4 decision was delivered by Chief Justice William Rehnquist, joined by Justices Antonin Scalia, Anthony Kennedy, and Clarence Thomas; Justice Stephen Breyer concurred, but wrote a separate opinion.

2. To be sure, Jesus identifies words early in the Shema ("You should love the Lord your God . . .") as the greatest commandment, followed by love of neighbor (Matthew 22:36–40; Mark 12:28–31; Luke 10:25–28). For monotheistic believers, the principle of love of God is self-evident, and also expresses another ideal articulated in the Decalogue: imitation of God, the freer of slaves, the father of the fatherless, the protector of widows, and the creator of all. But it should not be absolutized in the American context or in a pluralistic world.

SOURCES

Here are some of the works I found helpful in writing this book:

William P. Brown, ed., *The Ten Commandments: The Reciprocity of Faithfulness* (Louisville, KY: Westminster John Knox, 2004).

Raymond F. Collins, "Ten Commandments," pp. 383–87 in *The Anchor Bible Dictionary*, vol. 6 (ed. D. N. Freedman; New York: Doubleday, 1992).

Edgar W. Conrad, "From Jefferson's Bible to Judge Moore's Ten Commandments Monuments. Secularizing the Bible in the USA," pp. 162–77 in *Secularism and Biblical Studies* (ed. R. Boer; Oakville, CT: Equinox, 2010).

Matthias Köckert, *Die Zehn Gebote* (Munich: C. H. Beck, 2007).

Amy-Jill Levine and Marc Zvi Brettler, eds., *The Jewish Annotated New Testament* (New York: Oxford University Press, 2011)

Patrick D. Miller, *The Ten Commandments* (Louisville, KY: Westminster John Knox, 2009). A summary of Miller's conclusions is conveniently found in his entry "Ten Commandments," pp. 517–22 in *The New Interpreter's Dictionary of the Bible*, vol. 5 (ed. K. D. Sakenfeld; Nashville, TN: Abingdon, 2009).

Henning Graf Reventlow and Yair Hoffman, eds., *The Decalogue in Jewish and Christian Tradition* (New York: T & T Clark, 2011).

Ben-Zion Segal, ed., *The Ten Commandments in History and Tradition* (Jerusalem: Magnes Press, The Hebrew University of Jerusalem, 1990).

Johann Jakob Stamm and Maurice Edward Andrew, *The Ten Commandments in Recent Research* (London: SCM, 1967).

Moshe Weinfeld, "The Decalogue: Its Significance, Uniqueness, and Place in Israel's Tradition," pp. 3–47 in *Religion and Law: Biblical-Judaic and Islamic Perspectives* (ed. E. B. Firmage, B. G. Weiss, and J. W. Welch; Winona Lake, IN: Eisenbrauns, 1990).

ACKNOWLEDGMENTS

Many of the ideas in this book were developed while teaching a course in the Ten Commandments at Stonehill College; during it I learned much from my students, for which I am grateful. I also want to thank readers of my manuscript, especially two anonymous reviewers for Yale University Press. At Yale, Jennifer Banks has been an ideal editor—insightful, supportive, and patient. I also thank my agent, Stephen Hanselman, of LevelFiveMedia, for his ongoing enthusiasm for my work. Finally, as always, I am grateful to my family for their insightful and loving comments.

INDEX

Page numbers in *italic* type indicate illustrations. Page numbers
followed by t indicate a table. Page numbers followed by n indicate
an endnote.